HAFEZ
AL-ASSAD

HAFEZ AL-ASSAD

Matthew S. Gordon

CHELSEA HOUSE PUBLISHERS
NEW YORK
PHILADELPHIA

Chelsea House Publishers
EDITOR-IN-CHIEF: Nancy Toff
EXECUTIVE EDITOR: Remmel T. Nunn
MANAGING EDITOR: Karyn Gullen Browne
COPY CHIEF: Juliann Barbato
PICTURE EDITOR: Adrian G. Allen
ART DIRECTOR: Maria Epes
MANUFACTURING MANAGER: Gerald Levine

World Leaders—Past & Present
SENIOR EDITOR: John W. Selfridge

Staff for HAFEZ AL-ASSAD
ASSOCIATE EDITOR: Jeff Klein
ASSISTANT EDITOR: Terrance Dolan
COPY EDITOR: Philip Koslow
DEPUTY COPY CHIEF: Nicole Bowen
EDITORIAL ASSISTANTS: Heather Lewis, Nate Eaton
PICTURE RESEARCHER: Kathy Bonomi
ASSISTANT ART DIRECTOR: Loraine Machlin
DESIGNER: David Murray
DESIGN ASSISTANT: James Baker
PRODUCTION COORDINATOR: Joseph Romano
COVER ILLUSTRATION: Daniel O'Leary

First Printing

1 3 5 7 9 8 6 4 2

Library of Congress Cataloging in Publication Data

Gordon, Matthew.
  Hafez al-Assad / Matthew S. Gordon.
  p. cm.—(World leaders past & present)
  Bibliography: p.
  Includes index.
  Summary: A biography of the military leader who became
president of Syria in 1970.
  ISBN 1-55546-827-6
      0-7910-0672-7 (pbk.)
  1. Assad, Hafez, 1928–   —Juvenile literature.
2. Presidents—Syria—Biography—Juvenile literature. 3. Syria—
Politics and government—Juvenile literature. [1. Assad, Hafez,
1928–   . 2. Presidents—Syria. 3. Syria—Politics and
government.] I. Title. II. Series.
DS98.3.A8G67   1989
956.9104′2′092—dc19   89-7294
[B]   CIP
[92]   AC

Contents

JOHN ADAMS
JOHN QUINCY ADAMS
KONRAD ADENAUER
ALEXANDER THE GREAT
SALVADOR ALLENDE
MARC ANTONY
CORAZON AQUINO
YASIR ARAFAT
KING ARTHUR
HAFEZ AL-ASSAD
KEMAL ATATÜRK
ATTILA
CLEMENT ATTLEE
AUGUSTUS CAESAR
MENACHEM BEGIN
DAVID BEN-GURION
OTTO VON BISMARCK
LÉON BLUM
SIMON BOLÍVAR
CESARE BORGIA
WILLY BRANDT
LEONID BREZHNEV
JULIUS CAESAR
JOHN CALVIN
JIMMY CARTER
FIDEL CASTRO
CATHERINE THE GREAT
CHARLEMAGNE
CHIANG KAI-SHEK
WINSTON CHURCHILL
GEORGES CLEMENCEAU
CLEOPATRA
CONSTANTINE THE GREAT
HERNÁN CORTÉS
OLIVER CROMWELL
GEORGES-JACQUES
    DANTON
JEFFERSON DAVIS
MOSHE DAYAN
CHARLES DE GAULLE
EAMON DE VALERA
EUGENE DEBS
DENG XIAOPING
BENJAMIN DISRAELI
ALEXANDER DUBČEK
FRANÇOIS & JEAN-CLAUDE
    DUVALIER
DWIGHT EISENHOWER
ELEANOR OF AQUITAINE
ELIZABETH I
FAISAL
FERDINAND & ISABELLA
FRANCISCO FRANCO
BENJAMIN FRANKLIN

FREDERICK THE GREAT
INDIRA GANDHI
MOHANDAS GANDHI
GIUSEPPE GARIBALDI
AMIN & BASHIR GEMAYEL
GENGHIS KHAN
WILLIAM GLADSTONE
MIKHAIL GORBACHEV
ULYSSES S. GRANT
ERNESTO "CHE" GUEVARA
TENZIN GYATSO
ALEXANDER HAMILTON
DAG HAMMARSKJÖLD
HENRY VIII
HENRY OF NAVARRE
PAUL VON HINDENBURG
HIROHITO
ADOLF HITLER
HO CHI MINH
KING HUSSEIN
IVAN THE TERRIBLE
ANDREW JACKSON
JAMES I
WOJCIECH JARUZELSKI
THOMAS JEFFERSON
JOAN OF ARC
POPE JOHN XXIII
POPE JOHN PAUL II
LYNDON JOHNSON
BENITO JUÁREZ
JOHN KENNEDY
ROBERT KENNEDY
JOMO KENYATTA
AYATOLLAH KHOMEINI
NIKITA KHRUSHCHEV
KIM IL SUNG
MARTIN LUTHER KING, JR.
HENRY KISSINGER
KUBLAI KHAN
LAFAYETTE
ROBERT E. LEE
VLADIMIR LENIN
ABRAHAM LINCOLN
DAVID LLOYD GEORGE
LOUIS XIV
MARTIN LUTHER
JUDAS MACCABEUS
JAMES MADISON
NELSON & WINNIE
    MANDELA
MAO ZEDONG
FERDINAND MARCOS
GEORGE MARSHALL

MARY, QUEEN OF SCOTS
TOMÁŠ MASARYK
GOLDA MEIR
KLEMENS VON METTERNICH
JAMES MONROE
HOSNI MUBARAK
ROBERT MUGABE
BENITO MUSSOLINI
NAPOLÉON BONAPARTE
GAMAL ABDEL NASSER
JAWAHARLAL NEHRU
NERO
NICHOLAS II
RICHARD NIXON
KWAME NKRUMAH
DANIEL ORTEGA
MOHAMMED REZA PAHLAVI
THOMAS PAINE
CHARLES STEWART
    PARNELL
PERICLES
JUAN PERÓN
PETER THE GREAT
POL POT
MUAMMAR EL-QADDAFI
RONALD REAGAN
CARDINAL RICHELIEU
MAXIMILIEN ROBESPIERRE
ELEANOR ROOSEVELT
FRANKLIN ROOSEVELT
THEODORE ROOSEVELT
ANWAR SADAT
HAILE SELASSIE
PRINCE SIHANOUK
JAN SMUTS
JOSEPH STALIN
SUKARNO
SUN YAT-SEN
TAMERLANE
MOTHER TERESA
MARGARET THATCHER
JOSIP BROZ TITO
TOUSSAINT L'OUVERTURE
LEON TROTSKY
PIERRE TRUDEAU
HARRY TRUMAN
QUEEN VICTORIA
LECH WALESA
GEORGE WASHINGTON
CHAIM WEIZMANN
WOODROW WILSON
XERXES
EMILIANO ZAPATA
ZHOU ENLAI

CHELSEA HOUSE PUBLISHERS

ON LEADERSHIP

Arthur M. Schlesinger, jr.

LEADERSHIP, it may be said, is really what makes the world go round. Love no doubt smooths the passage; but love is a private transaction between consenting adults. Leadership is a public transaction with history. The idea of leadership affirms the capacity of individuals to move, inspire, and mobilize masses of people so that they act together in pursuit of an end. Sometimes leadership serves good purposes, sometimes bad; but whether the end is benign or evil, great leaders are those men and women who leave their personal stamp on history.

Now, the very concept of leadership implies the proposition that individuals can make a difference. This proposition has never been universally accepted. From classical times to the present day, eminent thinkers have regarded individuals as no more than the agents and pawns of larger forces, whether the gods and goddesses of the ancient world or, in the modern era, race, class, nation, the dialectic, the will of the people, the spirit of the times, history itself. Against such forces, the individual dwindles into insignificance.

So contends the thesis of historical determinism. Tolstoy's great novel *War and Peace* offers a famous statement of the case. Why, Tolstoy asked, did millions of men in the Napoleonic Wars, denying their human feelings and their common sense, move back and forth across Europe slaughtering their fellows? "The war," Tolstoy answered, "was bound to happen simply because it was bound to happen." All prior history predetermined it. As for leaders, they, Tolstoy said, "are but the labels that serve to give a name to an end and, like labels, they have the least possible connection with the event." The greater the leader, "the more conspicuous the inevitability and the predestination of every act he commits." The leader, said Tolstoy, is "the slave of history."

Determinism takes many forms. Marxism is the determinism of class. Nazism the determinism of race. But the idea of men and women as the slaves of history runs athwart the deepest human instincts. Rigid determinism abolishes the idea of human freedom—

the assumption of free choice that underlies every move we make, every word we speak, every thought we think. It abolishes the idea of human responsibility, since it is manifestly unfair to reward or punish people for actions that are by definition beyond their control. No one can live consistently by any deterministic creed. The Marxist states prove this themselves by their extreme susceptibility to the cult of leadership.

More than that, history refutes the idea that individuals make no difference. In December 1931 a British politician crossing Park Avenue in New York City between 76th and 77th Streets around 10:30 P.M. looked in the wrong direction and was knocked down by an automobile—a moment, he later recalled, of a man aghast, a world aglare: "I do not understand why I was not broken like an eggshell or squashed like a gooseberry." Fourteen months later an American politician, sitting in an open car in Miami, Florida, was fired on by an assassin; the man beside him was hit. Those who believe that individuals make no difference to history might well ponder whether the next two decades would have been the same had Mario Constasino's car killed Winston Churchill in 1931 and Giuseppe Zangara's bullet killed Franklin Roosevelt in 1933. Suppose, in addition, that Adolf Hitler had been killed in the street fighting during the Munich *Putsch* of 1923 and that Lenin had died of typhus during World War I. What would the 20th century be like now?

For better or for worse, individuals do make a difference. "The notion that a people can run itself and its affairs anonymously," wrote the philosopher William James, "is now well known to be the silliest of absurdities. Mankind does nothing save through initiatives on the part of inventors, great or small, and imitation by the rest of us—these are the sole factors in human progress. Individuals of genius show the way, and set the patterns, which common people then adopt and follow."

Leadership, James suggests, means leadership in thought as well as in action. In the long run, leaders in thought may well make the greater difference to the world. But, as Woodrow Wilson once said, "Those only are leaders of men, in the general eye, who lead in action. . . . It is at their hands that new thought gets its translation into the crude language of deeds." Leaders in thought often invent in solitude and obscurity, leaving to later generations the tasks of imitation. Leaders in action—the leaders portrayed in this series—have to be effective in their own time.

And they cannot be effective by themselves. They must act in response to the rhythms of their age. Their genius must be adapted, in a phrase of William James's, "to the receptivities of the moment." Leaders are useless without followers. "There goes the mob," said the French politician hearing a clamor in the streets. "I am their leader. I must follow them." Great leaders turn the inchoate emotions of the mob to purposes of their own. They seize on the opportunities of their time, the hopes, fears, frustrations, crises, potentialities. They succeed when events have prepared the way for them, when the community is awaiting to be aroused, when they can provide the clarifying and organizing ideas. Leadership ignites the circuit between the individual and the mass and thereby alters history.

It may alter history for better or for worse. Leaders have been responsible for the most extravagant follies and most monstrous crimes that have beset suffering humanity. They have also been vital in such gains as humanity has made in individual freedom, religious and racial tolerance, social justice, and respect for human rights.

There is no sure way to tell in advance who is going to lead for good and who for evil. But a glance at the gallery of men and women in *World Leaders—Past and Present* suggests some useful tests.

One test is this: Do leaders lead by force or by persuasion? By command or by consent? Through most of history leadership was exercised by the divine right of authority. The duty of followers was to defer and to obey. "Theirs not to reason why / Theirs but to do and die." On occasion, as with the so-called enlightened despots of the 18th century in Europe, absolutist leadership was animated by humane purposes. More often, absolutism nourished the passion for domination, land, gold, and conquest and resulted in tyranny.

The great revolution of modern times has been the revolution of equality. The idea that all people should be equal in their legal condition has undermined the old structure of authority, hierarchy, and deference. The revolution of equality has had two contrary effects on the nature of leadership. For equality, as Alexis de Tocqueville pointed out in his great study *Democracy in America*, might mean equality in servitude as well as equality in freedom.

"I know of only two methods of establishing equality in the political world," Tocqueville wrote. "Rights must be given to every citizen, or none at all to anyone . . . save one, who is the master of all." There was no middle ground "between the sovereignty of all and the absolute power of one man." In his astonishing prediction of 20th-century totalitarian dictatorship, Tocqueville explained how the revolution of equality could lead to the *"Führerprinzip"* and more terrible absolutism than the world had ever known.

But when rights are given to every citizen and the sovereignty of all is established, the problem of leadership takes a new form, becomes more exacting than ever before. It is easy to issue commands and enforce them by the rope and the stake, the concentration camp and the *gulag.* It is much harder to use argument and achievement to overcome opposition and win consent. The Founding Fathers of the United States understood the difficulty. They believed that history had given them the opportunity to decide, as Alexander Hamilton wrote in the first Federalist Paper, whether men are indeed capable of basing government on "reflection and choice, or whether they are forever destined to depend . . . on accident and force."

Government by reflection and choice called for a new style of leadership and a new quality of followership. It required leaders to be responsive to popular concerns, and it required followers to be active and informed participants in the process. Democracy does not eliminate emotion from politics; sometimes it fosters demagoguery; but it is confident that, as the greatest of democratic leaders put it, you cannot fool all of the people all of the time. It measures leadership by results and retires those who overreach or falter or fail.

It is true that in the long run despots are measured by results too. But they can postpone the day of judgment, sometimes indefinitely, and in the meantime they can do infinite harm. It is also true that democracy is no guarantee of virtue and intelligence in government, for the voice of the people is not necessarily the voice of God. But democracy, by assuring the right of opposition, offers built-in resistance to the evils inherent in absolutism. As the theologian Reinhold Niebuhr summed it up, "Man's capacity for justice makes democracy possible, but man's inclination to injustice makes democracy necessary."

A second test for leadership is the end for which power is sought. When leaders have as their goal the supremacy of a master race or the promotion of totalitarian revolution or the acquisition and exploitation of colonies or the protection of greed and privilege or the preservation of personal power, it is likely that their leadership will do little to advance the cause of humanity. When their goal is the abolition of slavery, the liberation of women, the enlargement of opportunity for the poor and powerless, the extension of equal rights to racial minorities, the defense of the freedoms of expression and opposition, it is likely that their leadership will increase the sum of human liberty and welfare.

Leaders have done great harm to the world. They have also conferred great benefits. You will find both sorts in this series. Even "good" leaders must be regarded with a certain wariness. Leaders are not demigods; they put on their trousers one leg after another just like ordinary mortals. No leader is infallible, and every leader needs to be reminded of this at regular intervals. Irreverence irritates leaders but is their salvation. Unquestioning submission corrupts leaders and demeans followers. Making a cult of a leader is always a mistake. Fortunately hero worship generates its own antidote. "Every hero," said Emerson, "becomes a bore at last."

The signal benefit the great leaders confer is to embolden the rest of us to live according to our own best selves, to be active, insistent, and resolute in affirming our own sense of things. For great leaders attest to the reality of human freedom against the supposed inevitabilities of history. And they attest to the wisdom and power that may lie within the most unlikely of us, which is why Abraham Lincoln remains the supreme example of great leadership. A great leader, said Emerson, exhibits new possibilities to all humanity. "We feed on genius. . . . Great men exist that there may be greater men."

Great leaders, in short, justify themselves by emancipating and empowering their followers. So humanity struggles to master its destiny, remembering with Alexis de Tocqueville: "It is true that around every man a fatal circle is traced beyond which he cannot pass; but within the wide verge of that circle he is powerful and free; as it is with man, so with communities."

1

"Everything Is Gone"

In February 1982, citizens of Syria's fourth-largest city, Hama, were about to witness one of the bloodiest episodes in the modern history of the Middle East, one in which thousands of people would die, fall wounded, or be driven from their homes.

For several years, Hama had been a center of resistance to Syria's ironhanded president, Hafez al-Assad. After a long period of political turmoil, Assad had seized power to become the nation's leader in 1970. His goals to promote Arab unity, oppose the Jewish state of Israel, and transform Syria into an economically sound socialist state were matched by his intense personal ambition. His primary concern was to stay in power, and in order to do so he had fought many difficult battles, both political and military. Despite opposition at home and abroad, Assad managed to maintain control of Syria.

In order to kill the revolution they will have to kill the people and this is impossible. They should know that Assad is no one but one of you. Every citizen in this country is Hafez al-Assad.
—HAFEZ AL-ASSAD

Residents of the western Syrian city of Hama wash wheat on the banks of the Orontes River during the 1950s near an ancient Roman aqueduct and a 14th-century waterwheel. In 1982, Muslim militants in Hama launched a revolt against the regime of Hafez al-Assad. Security forces under Assad's brother Rifat violently crushed the revolt.

The quiet, dignified Assad earned a reputation as a leader who combined stern pragmatism with perceptive cunning. He deployed an arsenal of diplomatic and economic tools to win support, but the real core of his power was the loyal backing he enjoyed from Syria's armed forces. Consequently, Assad could usually act as he saw fit, and, as the people of Hama would soon be reminded, when challenged he could be ruthless.

The Hama revolt was the culmination of the unrest that had plagued Assad's regime since the late 1970s. There had been numerous attacks by religious and political militants on government buildings and assassinations of prominent officials. By 1982 the government was facing something close to a popular uprising.

The reasons for this opposition are complex. For one thing, many Syrians resented the monopoly of political power held by Assad and a small circle of officials. Syrians were also bitter about the corruption present at every level of the government. But there were other, deeper reasons as well.

President Assad and many of the leaders of his government are members of a Muslim religious minority, the Alawis. When Assad first came to power the majority of Syrians, who were members of the long-dominant Sunni Muslim sect, were skeptical. As Assad established his regime, the Sunni community watched with growing resentment as the power of the Alawi minority grew. By 1980 almost all the top positions in both the government and military were in the hands of the Alawis, whereas the political strength of the Sunnis had sharply declined.

Economic troubles also fueled the opposition to Assad's regime. Hama had long been a center of small industry and trading, and many of the city's artisans and merchants felt threatened when Assad's government adopted economic programs that allowed cheap foreign goods to flood Syrian markets, cutting into the profits of local merchants. Thus, opposition to Assad's regime was rife in Hama by 1982. Consequently, when militants in the city staged an antigovernment uprising, they received strong support from the local populace.

Hama . . . had long been a redoubtable opponent of the Ba'thist state. By early 1982 relations between the city and the authorities in Damascus were inflamed, to say the least.
—PATRICK SEALE
journalist and
Assad biographer

The insurrection was spearheaded by members of a group known as the Ikhwan al-Muslimin, the Muslim Brotherhood. The Brotherhood was a political and religious organization founded in 1928 to promote the idea that the problems in present-day Arab society were attributable to a deviation from the teachings of Islam. In the eyes of these militants, Assad's regime was offensive since it sought to shape Syria into a secular, not a religious, state. In recent years the group had broken up into several large factions that disagreed on a number of issues. The most important of these was how best to challenge the Assad regime. The more radical factions — the militants who led the fight in Hama — had chosen armed resistance. In 1981 they staged strikes and demonstrations, and it was clear to many Syrians that they intended to escalate the conflict.

Members of the Muslim Brotherhood plan operations against the Assad regime in February 1982. The Brotherhood, which held that Syria should be ruled according to strict Islamic principles, believed that Assad's socialist government had turned the nation away from Islam.

In early 1982, government intelligence agents discovered that arms had been shipped to Brotherhood supporters in Hama. The local command decided to strike against the militants before these weapons were put to use. On the evening of February 2, a group of about 40 soldiers and intelligence agents moved into the narrow alleyways of old Hama. News of their operation, however, had been passed on to their intended victims. As the government forces approached their target, they walked into an ambush. In a few short minutes gunfire from members of the Brotherhood wiped out the entire raiding party.

Word of the ambush traveled quickly across Hama, sparking citywide revolt. Young men dashed to the mosques located within the old city. From the loudspeakers of the minarets — slender towers atop the mosques from which each day people are called to prayer — they denounced Assad and his government as irreligious and illegitimate oppressors. They urged the people of Hama to join them in armed revolt.

Meanwhile, their fellow militants moved against government and municipal targets. Late that night and early the next morning they stormed police stations, local army centers, government buildings, and other key locations. They were met with gunfire as local army units defended the rebels' targets. The rebels drove off these units and seized stores of arms and other goods. These supplies proved invaluable as the revolt continued to spread. Weapons were distributed to local supporters, and attacks on government and military buildings continued. Homes of local officials were attacked and scores of people were killed.

For the rebel leaders, all seemed to be going well. They had won the support of the townspeople, and they hoped that their local revolt would spark a national uprising. As news of the rebellion spread through the country, other cities might rise up, and the hated Assad regime would finally fall. However, the Muslim Brotherhood and their supporters had underestimated Assad's determination to remain in power.

At first, Assad had hoped that the uprising would die down quickly. He knew that if the military took the city by force many civilians were likely to be killed. Rather than further alienate the Syrian people from his government, Assad decided not to escalate the conflict by sending in reinforcements and instead considered entering into negotiations with the rebels. By the second day of the revolt, however, it was clear that the situation was even more serious than Assad had first imagined. Reports coming out of Hama indicated that the rebels were in virtual control of the city. And it was clear that they were in no mood to negotiate. One report issued by the Brotherhood dramatically proclaimed, "The people of Hama have risen in arms. . . . How has it happened? It was the only choice — the choice to save the nation."

Hama in March 1982. After the February takeover of Hama by the Muslim Brotherhood, government forces arrived to crush the revolt. Shelling buildings indiscriminately, they retook Hama and leveled most of the city's old quarter. Of Hama's 180,000 residents, as many as 30,000 may have been killed.

Syrian president Hafez al-Assad in 1983, one year after the Hama revolt. Having crushed active opposition to his regime Assad was then able to turn his attention to matters beyond his country's borders.

Assad realized that the rebellion could spread to other parts of the country, gravely threatening his regime. His government was also concerned that outside powers, including Syria's longtime enemy, Israel, might intervene on the side of the revolt. Another country hostile to the Assad government, Iraq, had already involved itself in the insurrection by broadcasting a rebel plea for a "civil mutiny" against the Assad regime. The president and his generals dropped the idea of negotiations. The time had come for the government to send the clear message to its opponents both within and outside Syria that Hafez al-Assad intended to remain in control.

In Hama the fighting intensified. Local military units continued to engage the rebels, and large numbers of reinforcements were flown into the city. Two units were selected — the 21st Mechanized Infantry Brigade and the 47th Independent Armored Brigade. They were accompanied by crack units of the *Saraya al-difa'* (Defense Companies), an elite branch of the army commanded by Rifat al-Assad, the president's brother. In all, approximately 7,000 soldiers were sent in to quell the uprising.

The center of the rebellion was the al-Hadhir quarter, located in the old city. According to eyewitness accounts, government tanks and artillery pounded the neighborhood with shells. Helicopters circled above the area, firing down upon the rebels. Four Japanese businessmen, fleeing the escalating violence, reported seeing a force of more than 100 tanks barraging rebel strongholds from the southern bank of the Orontes River, which flows through the city.

After a period of heavy shelling the government decided to send in infantry units to clear out the rebels. But Assad's generals had underestimated the determination and popular support of the Brotherhood. The fighting continued for days. Government soldiers, fighting in the unfamiliar, twisting alleys of the old city, found themselves up against locals who knew the city well. Assad's troops resorted to intense firepower to compensate for this disadvantage. Machine-gun fire cut down civilians along with rebel fighters, and explosions devastated entire neighborhoods.

As the days wore on, the conflict was reduced to house-to-house battles. According to one Syrian soldier, the resistance continued to be impassioned: "I saw the doors and windows of the houses opened and the people shouted '*Allahu akbar* [God is great]. Go away, murderers, we want Islam.'" Government troops, faced with the fervent determination of their opponents, resorted to brutal tactics. Witnesses to the fighting reported later that the soldiers often responded to sniper fire by simply destroying entire floors or even buildings to stop the firing. These tactics led to increasing numbers of civilian casualties. The resistance was no match for the heavily armed soldiers, and by February 14, Assad's army had reestablished control over most of Hama.

Fearful that the rebellion might spread, Syrian officials had suppressed reports coming out of Hama and consistently denied that anything unusual was taking place there. It was only on February 23 that the regime finally issued its first official statement on the events in Hama. Assad's government accused the Muslim Brotherhood of having started the fighting by savagely murdering local government representatives and their families. To prevent further "atrocities," security forces had been obliged to carry out a "police action." The statement concluded by saying that the "criminals" had been punished and would never again carry out such activities.

The full extent of the destruction in Hama will never be known, nor will the number of dead. So many of the dead were buried in the rubble of destroyed buildings that it is impossible to arrive at an accurate figure. Estimates range between 5,000 and 30,000 killed.

Months later an American journalist, Thomas Friedman, was permitted into Hama along with other reporters. In an article for the *New York Times* he characterized Hama as "a broken city." The effects of the fighting were present everywhere. Whole areas of the old city had been leveled. When a middle-aged resident was asked what had happened to his neighborhood he responded simply, "Everything is gone."

One Arab nation with an eternal message.
—Ba'th party slogan

2
Choosing a Path

Hafez al-Assad was born on October 6, 1930, in Qardaha, a small village near the city of Latakia in northwestern Syria. At birth he was named Abu Sulayman, after his grandfather Sulayman, reportedly a brave patriot and soldier. Abu Sulayman's family name was Wahsh, the Arabic word for wild beast. When he was a teenager, this name was changed to Assad, which means lion. The new name would suit its proud bearer very well, although some would argue that the first was more apt.

Assad's family was typical of Latakia province, a rural area that derived its name from its most important city, the port city of Latakia. His father, Ali Wahsh, was a small landowner who supported his family through farming. Despite the difficulties of living off the land, Ali Wahsh managed well in providing for his wife and children. Assad was the eldest of eight children—six boys and two girls.

The use of force and violence against my people convinced me that military service would be the most effective way to serve [them].
—HAFEZ AL-ASSAD

The Sitt Zeinab Mosque outside Damascus, the capital of Syria. One of the world's oldest cities, Damascus was conquered by the Arabs in A.D. 635 and has been one of the most important centers of the Islamic world ever since.

21

Like most of the people living in the areas surrounding Latakia, the Wahsh family were members of the Alawi sect. Although the Alawis were a majority in the northwest, within all of Syria they formed a small minority, about 12 percent of the population. The Wahsh family, like their neighbors, came to know the frustrations that came with being members of a minority.

The history of the Alawi sect is a complex one. There is much that is not known about the group. They were originally called the al-Nusayriyah, a name which was later given to the rugged Latakia mountain range where many of them lived. The origin of this name is unclear; it may have come from the name of a 9th-century Muslim scholar, Muhammad ibn Nusayr.

The al-Nusayriyah, or the Nusayris, held a set of beliefs that were seen by other Muslims as offensive. Islam, like Christianity and Judaism, incorporates a number of sects that profess distinct doctrines while agreeing on certain fundamental beliefs. The two largest Muslim sects, the Sunnis and the Shi'a, believed that the Nusayris deviated from the Islamic tradition. Some Sunnis and Shi'ites maintained that they were not even Muslim.

One fundamental belief shared by both the Sunnis and the Shi'a concerns the nature of God. Like Christianity and Judaism, Islam is a monotheistic religion. This means that Muslims, whether they are Sunnis or Shi'ites, believe in the existence of one and only one god. The Nusayris apparently held an opposing doctrine. Drawing partly on ancient Syrian beliefs, they worshiped many gods, including the sun, moon, and sky. They also believed that certain divine figures had appeared on earth in human form. To Syria's Sunni majority, the Nusayris violated the monotheism on which Islam was based.

Among the persons most revered by the Nusayris was Ali ibn Abu Talib. Ali, who died in A.D. 661, was a close companion of Muhammad, the prophet and founder of the Islamic religion. Ali is considered an important historical figure by all Muslims. The Nusayris went further. They said that Ali was divine. It is probably because of this belief in the divine

Founded as a religious sect apparently during the late tenth century . . . the Nusayris—later known as Alawis or Alawites—have professed an esoteric secret faith.

—MOSHE MA'OZ
Assad biographer

nature of Ali that the Nusayris have come to be called the Alawis.

Religious differences separated the Alawi sect from Syria's Sunni majority, but a variety of factors contributed to this isolation. Geography, for instance, played a role in maintaining the Alawis' distinct identity. The al-Nusayriyah mountains blocked easy access between northwestern Syria and the rest of the country. In addition, social and economic divisions played a role. The Sunnis of northern Syria were mostly middle- and upper-class urban dwellers who worked as artisans or merchants. They generally looked down on the Alawis, many of whom were impoverished, illiterate peasants. For centuries there was little real contact between the two populations.

As a distinct minority, the Alawis developed their own traditions and customs. Among these were a strong sense of self-reliance and loyalty to their own community. These qualities served the Alawis well in the face of outside threats.

Despite its isolation, the Alawi region was not spared outside invasion. Over the centuries a series of armies have conquered the area. Generally these powers had little interest in the Alawis themselves.

Muslims read at a Damascus mosque. Like the majority of the world's Muslims, most Syrians belong to Islam's Sunni sect. About 11 percent of all Syrians, including Assad, belong to the Alawi sect, which mixes Islamic and pre-Islamic beliefs, and another 3 percent are Druze. About 13 percent of all Syrians are Christian.

They asked only that they submit to the central state, which usually meant paying unreasonably high taxes. This was galling to the independent, self-sufficient Alawis; whenever they could, they rose in revolt. This fierce resistance to outside control was passed on from generation to generation.

At the time of Assad's birth the Alawis were still fairly isolated. Many of his people remained poor and uneducated. They often worked on the estates of urban landowners who exploited the villagers as cheap laborers. Though there were some Alawis and Christians among these landowners, the majority were Sunnis. Their exploitation of the Alawis deepened the divisions between Syria's Alawi and Sunni populations.

The Wahsh family was better off than many. Because Ali Wahsh owned his own farm, he was not at the mercy of wealthy landowners. In contrast to many of his fellow Alawis, he was also well educated, which left him better equipped to deal with the problems that he and his family faced. In several important ways Ali Wahsh helped form the attitudes that would govern his eldest son's life.

As an adult, Hafez al-Assad claimed that his father had been one of the greatest influences in his life. He spoke, for example, of Ali Wahsh's passion for Arabic poetry and history. Through stories, Ali Wahsh informed his children about the great episodes and figures of the Arab past. He also taught them about the history of the Alawis and encouraged them to appreciate the traditions of their community. In this way he instilled in his offspring a pride in their Alawi heritage and an interest in the history of the larger Arab world.

From his father and his classes at elementary school, Assad learned a great deal about the complex history of the region known today as the nation of Syria. At the start of the 16th century, much of the Middle East came under the control of the Ottoman Turks. Syria remained part of the Ottoman Empire for 400 years. During much of that time the region was governed by rulers who treated their subjects harshly. The Alawis in northwestern Syria were especially hard hit under Ottoman rule. Many were reduced to abject poverty by exorbitant taxes.

The Alawis were hostile to the Turks from the start. The natural resentment a subject people felt for their rulers was heightened by religious differences: The Ottomans were Sunnis who disapproved of Alawi beliefs. On a number of occasions the Alawis turned to outright revolt. This usually meant refusing to pay taxes to their Ottoman overlords. These uprisings were often brutally repressed.

World War I finally drove the Turks out of Syria. A few months after war broke out in 1914, the Ottoman Empire joined the conflict on the side of Germany and Austria-Hungary, who were fighting against Great Britain, France, and Russia. In 1916, to strengthen its efforts against the Turks, the British encouraged the Arabs to revolt. The person they asked to lead the rebellion was Amir Husayn, the head of a powerful family descended from the prophet Muhammad.

A group of Alawi peasants, circa 1900. Centered mainly in the northwest province of Latakia, the Alawis lived for centuries in near isolation from the rest of Syria. On a number of occasions, especially in the Ottoman period, the Alawis rebelled against the central authorities.

Troops of Emir Faisal's Arab army in Damascus stand in formation in 1920. British-backed Arab forces, led by Faisal, had driven the Ottomans out of Syria during World War I. The British had promised Faisal that his country would be rewarded with its independence, but in 1918 they supported French claims to Syria.

The British promised Husayn they would support the creation of independent Arab states after the war if the Arabs rose up against the Ottomans. Husayn agreed, and the revolt was launched in June 1916. Arab guerrillas waged a relentless war against the already embattled Ottomans. The revolt ended when the Turks decided to withdraw their troops from the Arab lands. On September 30, 1918, Arab troops entered Damascus, where they were joyfully greeted by the general populace. Four hundred years of Ottoman rule had come to an end. Many Syrians believed that independence had finally been won.

They soon learned, however, that Great Britain would not honor the bargain it had struck to gain Arab support. In 1916, Britain and France had signed the Sykes-Picot Agreement, a secret pact that stipulated that they would divide most of the Middle East once the Ottomans were driven out of the region. The British had signed this agreement before promising Amir Husayn that they would support Arab independence.

As World War I drew to a close the terms of the Sykes-Picot Agreement finally became known. Part of Syria would come under French rule, and the rest of the nation would be in the French "zone of influence," which meant indirect rule. Once again, Syria was threatened with takeover by an outside power.

Determined to resist the French, the Syrians decided to form a permanent government out of the provisional government that had been set up in 1918 under Faisal, one of Husayn's sons.

In March 1920, delegates to a national congress proclaimed Faisal king of Syria. France, predictably, voiced loud objections to this political move. Four months later French troops based on the Syrian coast marched on the nation's capital, Damascus. After defeating a small Arab force, they entered the city and deposed King Faisal.

That same year Britain and France announced the creation of the mandate system, the final step in the establishment of British and French control over much of the Middle East. According to this system the two European states would govern the region while helping the former Ottoman colonies to prepare for self-government. Both nations ignored Arab protests that the region was already long overdue for self-rule. Great Britain and France opted to treat their former allies in the Middle East as a conquered peoples. The British mandate extended over Iraq, Jordan, and Palestine. The French, in turn, set up their mandate in Syria.

One of the first decisions made by the French was to carve Syria up into separate units. One of these was called Greater Lebanon, which would become modern-day Lebanon. The other units included separate areas for the Alawis and the Druze, another of the region's religious minorities. To many observers both inside and outside Syria, the French policy looked like a deliberate attempt to weaken opposition by dividing the country. By giving the Alawis and the Druze their own areas, the French seemed to be trying to keep them from banding together with the Sunnis to resist French domination.

As the French consolidated their control the nationalist movement in Syria grew rapidly. This movement had emerged at the end of the 19th century, when Arab intellectuals had begun to speak of the Arab "nation." They argued that because the Arabs spoke a common language, had common traditions, and shared a common history, they should form a distinct political unit.

French generals lead their occupation forces into Beirut, Lebanon, in 1914. Six years later, after defeating Faisal's forces at Damascus, the French occupied Syria, which at the time included what is today Lebanon. The British, meanwhile, established control over the territory that currently comprises Israel, Jordan, and Iraq.

The nationalist movement gained momentum in the early 20th century. The struggle then was against the Ottoman Turks. Small political societies sprang up across Syria to attain the goal of national independence. During the Arab Revolt of World War I, these societies assisted Britain and France in pushing the Turks out of Syria. After the war, the nationalists faced a new opponent: the French.

The Wahsh clan, like many Alawi families, had a long tradition of opposing foreign rule. Assad's grandfather, according to family legend, had fought against the Turks. His father, Ali Wahsh, now opposed French rule. He worked with other nationalists to organize resistance in the Latakia region. Although it is not known whether or not he took part in any military activities, he acquired a reputation as a political activist.

In the late 1930s and early 1940s the nationalist movement continued to spread as Syrians of all religious persuasions struggled to force the French out of their country. Assad was too young to have joined the movement, but as he testified in later years, his father's passionate nationalism deeply impressed him. The memory of his father's activities against the French probably inspired him in later years, when he plunged into politics himself.

Ali Wahsh influenced his son in another way. He himself had benefited from formal education, and was convinced that academic training would improve the prospects of his children. Despite his limited income, he did all he could to provide them with decent education.

Assad began his schooling in Qardaha with five years of study at the local *kuttab*, or Koran school (the Koran is the holy book of Islam). Like most Muslim children, he learned to read and write by reciting and copying out verses from the Koran. At the age of 14 he left the village and went to Latakia. There his parents enrolled him in a preparatory school where he completed his primary education.

Assad remained at the Latakia school for his secondary education. A hardworking young man, he attracted the attention of his teachers and peers and became one of the top pupils in his class. As his popularity rose he went on to become a student leader. Like so many other Arab youths of his generation, he also became deeply involved in politics. According to Majid Khadduri, a scholar who has written on Assad, "It was fashionable in those days that students often took to the street in support of popular demands, as students in Syria — indeed, in many other Arab countries — had become highly politicized."

Hafez al-Assad celebrated his 16th birthday in 1946, the same year that Syrian nationalists claimed victory over France. After struggling for two decades, the Syrian leadership had finally achieved its goal. France had tried hard to retain at least indirect control over the country. But the French government had finally given in to pressures from the Syrian nationalists, who were supported by Great Britain, the United States, and the Soviet Union. The last French troops departed Syria on April 17, 1946.

The long battle for self-determination had been won, but new challenges lay ahead. Syrian leaders now faced the daunting task of creating a stable nation. Except for the two brief years in 1918–1920 when Faisal headed the country, the region had not experienced self-government for centuries. To make the task even more difficult, internal political divisions were mounting.

> *The army was an attractive alternative because, since independence in 1946, fees had been abolished at the military academy at Homs which thus became the only institution to offer poor boys a start in life: the cadets were lodged, fed, and even paid to be there.*
> —PATRICK SEALE
> journalist and
> Assad biographer

The nationalist movement in Syria had never been well united. From the early 1930s on a number of political parties emerged from within the movement. Each of these had its own platform. As long as the French were present these parties had a common goal, but once they left, the disagreements between these factions burst into the open.

The importance of these political events was not lost on Hafez al-Assad. Nor did it fail to fascinate him. First at home, and now in school, he was surrounded by political discussions and activity. As a student leader he was now taking part in rallies and demonstrations. He also gave several speeches in which he addressed issues concerning Syria and the rest of the Arab world.

After his graduation from secondary school Assad was ready to begin the next phase of his life. He was anxious to continue both his education and his political activities. For a young Alawi of limited income the choices were few. Most of the students studying law or medicine at the top universities were Sunnis from wealthy backgrounds. Most Alawis chose to apply to either Syria's teachers college or the military academy.

Soldiers watch over crowds at a Damascus religious festival in the early 1940s. The Syrian nationalist movement strongly opposed French rule. In 1946, one year after the conclusion of World War II, the French pulled out and granted Syria its independence.

Assad did not hesitate long in making his decision. The military academy was by far the better school. In addition, military training would provide him with some high-level technical skills. Like many other members of religious minorities, he was also attracted by the likelihood that in the military he would be judged on merit rather than on faith. Largely for this reason, by the 1950s the Alawi community was well represented in the armed forces.

Because the Syrian military was closely involved in government, Assad also hoped that a career in the army might allow him to pursue his interest in politics. Aware of his nation's troubled past, he was committed to doing all he could to help secure its future. Years later, Assad told a London *Times* reporter, "The use of force and violence against my people convinced me that military service would be the most effective way to serve my country."

With his strong personality and excellent academic record, Assad was an attractive candidate for admission to any school, and in 1952 he was accepted by the military academy at Homs. This was the start of what would become a distinguished military career. More important, it was Hafez al-Assad's first step toward political power.

An early meeting of the Arab League, an organization of newly independent Arab nations founded in 1946. Its charter members were Syria, Saudi Arabia, Egypt, Iraq, Jordan, Lebanon, and the Yemen Arab Republic.

3

Restless Birth of Two Nations

Hafez al-Assad's youth was shaped by his country's struggle against the French, who had governed Syria under a mandate system that was in effect from 1920 to 1946. His adulthood, however, would be deeply influenced by France's partner in the Middle Eastern mandate system — Great Britain. Although Syria itself would not be directly affected by Great Britain's mandate, the decisions made in dismantling British colonial rule in the region would profoundly affect the entire Middle East for decades to come.

Under the mandate system instituted after World War I, the region known as Palestine had come under British control in 1920. Just as had happened in Syria, the area's Arabs formed a nationalist movement to demand an end to foreign rule. The Palestinian nationalists soon found that they faced resistance not only from the British but also from an even more determined enemy — the Zionist movement.

The rise of Israel to statehood and the consequent inability of Arab states to prevent its expansion provided another compelling reason for unity, not only among the dismembered parts of geographical Syria but also among other Arab countries.
—MAJID KHADDURI
professor of
political science

Arab demonstrators throw rocks at British troops in Jaffa, Palestine, during the 1936 clashes between the Arabs and the British. The struggle over Palestine would grow over the next few decades into the Arab-Israeli conflict, in which Syria and its Arab neighbors would fight four major wars with Israel.

Theodor Herzl (seated, second row, third from left), one of the founders of the Zionist movement, with other Zionist leaders in 1902. The movement brought Jews, fleeing the anti-Semitism of Europe, to settle in Palestine, which had been the Jewish homeland from biblical times until the 2nd century A.D.

Zionism was established in the late 19th century by Jewish political activists in Europe. The principal goal of this movement was the creation of a Jewish state in Palestine. The Zionists had been deeply influenced by ideas sweeping across Europe in that period. Perhaps the most important of these ideas was the belief that all peoples sharing a common language and heritage had a right to their own sovereign state. The Zionists believed that Jews had been denied this right and that it was improbable that Jews could ever find a home in Europe. They pointed to the anti-Semitism in England, France, Russia, eastern Europe, and Germany as proof. Only in their own nation, they said, could the Jewish people prosper. Palestine was where they vowed to build this new nation.

In the first decades of the 20th century, Zionist leaders struggled to win the support of the British government. One result of this lobbying was the Balfour Declaration. Issued in November 1917, this was an official announcement by the British government that it supported the creation of a Jewish homeland in Palestine.

Even before the Balfour Declaration, Jewish immigrants from Europe had begun to establish small settlements in Palestine, and their numbers increased slowly but steadily. Although the immigrants remained a small minority, their activities aroused the resentment of the Arab majority. After the Balfour Declaration was issued, tensions increased. It was clear to the Palestinians that Great Britain was helping the Zionists seize part if not all of Palestine in order to establish this new Jewish homeland.

As Jewish immigration continued, violence erupted. Clashes between Arabs and Jews occurred in the late 1920s and early 1930s. Zionist organizations in the United States and Europe shipped arms to the Jewish settlers in Palestine, aggravating the already tense situation.

The British took measures to maintain order. They also tried to find ways to reach a compromise between the two communities. To satisfy Arab demands, for example, the British restricted Jewish immigration and limited land purchases by the Zionists. These measures proved ineffective, angering the Zionists and failing to placate the Arabs.

Finally, in April 1936, an Arab uprising erupted in Palestine. Clashes in Jaffa left 2 Arabs and 11 Jews dead. The violence spread and soon turned into a full-scale revolt by the Palestinians against British rule and the activities of the Zionist movement. A general strike was organized by Arab leaders, and throughout Palestine, Arabs fought British troops backed by Jewish irregulars. The uprising captured the attention of the entire Arab world. As Tabitha Petran, the author of *Syria*, put it: "The Palestine rebellion became the focus of a common Arab struggle for liberation and gave a new meaning to the ideas of Arab nationalism."

Syria, in the broad historical-geographical sense of the term, is the home of the founding fathers of Arab nationalism and became in the subsequent development of the nationalist movement the fountain of that movement.
—MAJID KHADDURI
professor of political science

By 1939 the rebellion, which was waged sporadically despite the influx of 20,000 additional British troops into the region, was finally over. More than 1,000 Arabs, along with 80 Jews and 37 British, were dead. Little had been resolved, and fighting between Arabs and Jews was growing more intense. Jewish militia staged attacks on Palestinian villages in the hopes of frightening Arabs out of Palestine. In many cases the strategy was successful, and thousands of villagers fled their homes. Arab militants, in turn, attacked Jewish settlements. Great Britain's attempts to reach an accord satisfied neither the Zionists nor the Palestinians. In 1947, Britain, severely taxed by World War II and weary of its attempts to restore order in the troubled Middle East, announced that it was withdrawing from Palestine.

The problems facing the Palestinians were now placed in the hands of the United Nations, a newly created multinational organization dedicated to resolving international disputes. On November 29, 1947, the UN approved a plan that would divide Palestine into two independent states — one Jewish, one Arab. Convinced that all of Palestine was rightfully theirs, most Palestinians resisted the partition plan.

A 1936 meeting of Palestinian and other Arab leaders in Jerusalem during the Arab uprising against the British colonial government and the Zionist movement. The uprising was sparked by the rising number of settlers, by their demands for an independent Jewish state in Palestine, and by British assurances that Jews would be granted such a state.

Jewish refugees from Europe await British permission to land at Haifa, Palestine, in 1946, soon after the end of World War II. German forces systematically killed 6 million Jews during the war; when the extent of the atrocities became known, worldwide pressure to allow the establishment of a Jewish state in Palestine increased.

Events in Palestine came to a head on May 15, 1948, when Great Britain pulled the last of its troops out of the region and Zionist leaders proclaimed the creation of the state of Israel. In response, Syria and other Arab states mobilized military forces to support the Palestinians. In the eyes of most Arab leaders, the new Jewish state was illegitimate, and its creation had to be opposed. The Arab-Israeli conflict had begun.

Although several Arab nations — including Syria, Egypt, Iraq, and Saudi Arabia — sent troops into Palestine, these forces soon realized that the battle would not be an easy one. The Arab leaders involved were more concerned with maneuvering for power at home than with Palestine's political situation, so their commitment to the fighting was weak, and most battalions were underequipped. The Israeli forces, on the other hand, were well armed and were supported by a wealthy superpower, the United States. By early 1949 the small Arab forces were defeated.

Jewish residents of Jerusalem stand behind barbed wire marking the boundary between the Jewish and Arab zones of the city in 1947. In that year the United Nations voted, over Arab objections, to divide Palestine into separate Arab and Jewish states.

Like most other Syrians, young Hafez al-Assad was deeply interested in the events taking place in Palestine. He was by this time a committed Arab nationalist who felt that the problems facing the Arab world would only be resolved when the Arabs were free of foreign domination and were united politically. To these nationalists, the nation of Israel had been unfairly carved out of territory that rightfully belonged to Palestinian Arabs. Assad would remain a committed enemy of the Jewish state long after he became Syria's president.

The creation of Israel was not the only political development that captured Assad's attention in the late 1940s. Syria itself was experiencing political and social upheaval. In 1949 alone, the government was overthrown three times by military coups. Demonstrations and strikes by labor unions and other organizations were occurring regularly. These groups charged that the Syrian government was a corrupt, reactionary group of politicians more interested in maintaining power than in addressing the needs of the country.

When Syria secured its independence in 1946, the government was dominated by a small group of upper-class conservative politicians. Most of these leaders were Sunni merchants, large landowners, and industrialists. As committed nationalists, these men had provided leadership in the fight against the French. Once independence was won, they kept their hold on political power. Unfortunately, it soon became obvious that they were not going to lead the country as well as they had led the nationalist struggle. These leaders were either unable or unwilling to respond to the rapid social and economic changes taking place in Syria. They tended to see reform as a threat to their power and wealth, so they resisted demands for change. In order to silence their opponents, they frequently resorted to censorship and political repression.

Despite efforts to still them, new voices began to be heard in Syrian politics. Dynamic young leaders espoused new ideas, often forming their own political parties. Although these parties disagreed on many issues, they shared a distrust of the traditional leadership. They accused the older leaders of not having done enough to support the Palestinians. These young activists also accused the government of corruption and repression. They argued that real change could only come after the conservative leadership stepped aside.

These new political currents swept through the Alawi community with great force. Most affected was the new generation of Alawis. Unlike their parents, many of these young Alawis were well educated. With their education came a new awareness of the world and their place in it. Seeking new opportunities, many of them, including Hafez al-Assad, looked to the military.

Through the 1950s the Homs Military Academy graduated large numbers of Alawis. At that time they were restricted to the lower and middle ranks of the officer corps, whereas the top positions in most branches of the military were held by Sunnis. One exception to this rule was the air force. In 1950 and 1952, Alawi officers were selected as commanders of this small but growing branch of the armed forces.

The ruins of bombed buildings in Jerusalem in 1948. On November 29, 1947, the UN voted to support the creation of a Jewish state in part of Palestine. This was followed by the declaration of Israel's independence by the Zioinist leader David Ben-Gurion on May 14, 1948.

Inspired by the example of these Alawi commanders, Assad transferred from the Homs Military Academy to the Air Force Academy in Aleppo in either 1953 or 1954. He proved to be an excellent pilot. At his graduation in 1955 he was awarded the best aviator trophy. He then went to Egypt, where he continued his training as a combat pilot.

Two years later, Hafez al-Assad was promoted from lieutenant to squadron commander. He was sent to the Soviet Union for further specialized training in combat aircraft. Both in Egypt and in the Soviet Union, Assad continued to win prizes for his skills as a pilot. He also built up important contacts among his fellow officers. The time was drawing near when he would put these contacts to valuable use.

Despite his achievements in the air force, Assad was seldom distracted from politics. He was now involved in the activities of a small political group, the Ba'th (Renaissance) party. The Ba'th was one of several new organizations that were challenging the

power of the traditional Sunni leadership. The party was significant for two reasons: First, it was developing strong links with the military; second, it boasted a large Alawi membership.

The Ba'th had emerged from the Arab nationalist movement. It was the creation of Michel Aflaq, an Orthodox Christian, and Salah al-Din al-Bitar, a Sunni Muslim. Both men had begun their political activities as schoolteachers in Damascus. They had first met in Paris, where they were studying at the Sorbonne. After returning to Syria in 1934 they set about forming a political organization. The first Ba'th party congress, held in April 1946, laid down the basic tenets of Ba'thism.

Aflaq and Bitar based their party platform on several key ideas, which are summarized in the Ba'th slogan, Unity, Freedom, and Socialism. Party doctrine holds that all the countries in the Arab world should join together to form one nation, free from all outside domination or interference. To these ideas Aflaq and Bitar added socialist doctrines they had learned in France. Socialism, they felt, was the foundation upon which to build the new Arab nation. Instead of a free market economy, which Aflaq and Bitar felt exploited workers, they envisioned a government-controlled economic system, which they hoped would bring both prosperity and equality.

The Ba'th won support in various parts of the Middle East. Parties were set up in Lebanon, Jordan, and Iraq as well as in Syria. In both Iraq and Syria the Ba'th would eventually come to power. In Syria, the party attracted young people from both the Sunni and the minority communities. For these minorities, the ideas of the Ba'th were especially attractive. Aflaq and Bitar's new brand of nationalism was secular, unlike traditional Arab unity movements, which were mostly led by Sunni Muslims. The Ba'th party leaders were not interested in the religious background of their followers, but in their commitment to their Arab identity.

Arab prisoners of war in an Israeli stockade in 1949, after Israel defeated the Arab League forces. The events of 1947—48 forced tens of thousands of Palestinian Arabs to leave Palestine, which had been their homeland for centuries. The Palestinians have been the focus of conflict in the Middle East ever since.

A 1957 photo of Salah al-Din al-Bitar, a cofounder of the Syrian Ba'th party. Advocating Syrian nationalism, Arab unity, and a socialist economic system, the Ba'thists quickly gained strength among young Syrians, including Assad, an air force officer who was recognized at the time as one of Syria's top combat pilots.

The Ba'th party articulated the grievances of Syria's middle and lower classes while challenging the leadership of the Sunni elite. According to the founders of the party, "We came from the people and shared their misfortunes." In contrast, they portrayed Syria's conservative rulers as corrupt and self-serving leaders who had little interest in the needs of the Syrian people.

After 1948, Ba'th leaders also accused the traditional elite of having betrayed the Arabs of Palestine by not doing enough to oppose the creation of Israel. The new Jewish state, they said, was a threat to Arab unity. The Ba'th party insisted on a new and more aggressive policy toward Israel.

Assad joined the Ba'th in the mid-1940s and quickly began to move up in its ranks. In 1947 he was assigned to head a new student unit of the Ba'th in Latakia. He continued his activities with the party after entering the military. It was, however, only after his graduation from the Air Force Academy in 1955 that Assad turned to full-time activity with the Ba'th. Within two years his activities with the party would put him at the center of Arab politics.

4

Humiliation and Power

At the start of the 1950s, Syrian political life was in turmoil. Unions, student groups, and political parties were regularly taking to the streets to protest government corruption and mismanagement.

Since 1949, the Syrian government had been headed by a high-ranking Sunni officer, Colonel Adib al-Shishakli. Until 1951 he had let civilian politicians shape most of his government's policies. As civil unrest increased, however, Shishakli grew worried and decided to consolidate his power. In December 1951 he ousted the civilians from the government. The new regime he created was essentially a military dictatorship. Shishakli dissolved parliament, outlawed all political parties, and took other repressive measures.

Syria's sacrifices are clear and bright. She is sacrificing her sons, economy, land and everything so that the Palestinian question may continue . . . and ultimately restore our [Israeli] occupied land and the rights of our displaced people.
—HAFEZ AL-ASSAD
on Syria's support of the
Palestinian movement

A crowd gathers around a bonfire in Aleppo, Syria's second-largest city, during the 1954 coup that toppled the five-year-old military government of Col. Adib al-Shishakli. The ensuing elections left the Ba'th party in power — and started Assad on the road to political prominence.

Former president Shishakli in exile in Switzerland three years after his overthrow. From 1949 until 1951 he headed a civilian government, but after strikes and protests against government corruption he dissolved the parliament and outlawed political organizations, including the Ba'th party.

Along with other parties, the Ba'th was outlawed during this period, but its leaders continued to develop new ideas — and win new recruits — by continuing their activities in secret. Faced with the threat of arrest, Aflaq and Bitar fled to Lebanon in December 1952. There they were joined by a third Syrian, Akram Hawrani. Hawrani was one of the upcoming young political leaders of this period. Like Aflaq and Bitar, he had a strong belief in both Arab nationalism and socialism. In the 1940s, Hawrani had begun to organize the peasantry to fight against exploitation by large landowners. He gained a large following in the rural areas around Hama, and in 1945 he organized a political movement called the Arab Socialist party. Now that his party was banned and he was in exile, he agreed to join forces with Aflaq and Bitar. This was an important step for the Ba'th. Because of his popularity in the peasant and military communities, Hawrani greatly expanded the Ba'th party's political strength.

In 1954 the Ba'th joined a coalition of parties that forced Shishakli to step down. The coalition restored constitutional rule and called for a popular election. Demonstrating its new popularity, the Ba'th party won 22 seats in parliament. But neither the Ba'th party nor any other political group was able to resolve the tensions that were dividing the country. Leftist factions, such as the Ba'th and the Syrian Communist party, were opposed by conservative forces, which were supported by the United States and Turkey. Violence between rival factions seemed imminent. The leaders of the Ba'th and their supporters in the military agreed that a solution had to be found quickly. The one they chose was union with Egypt.

Egypt was then ruled by Gamal Abdel Nasser. For the Ba'th and their supporters in the military, union with Nasser was an attractive prospect. Ba'thist ideology was firmly based on the idea of unity between the Arab states. In addition, Nasser was the Arab world's most popular and influential leader. With his support, the Ba'th leaders hoped they could bring an end to the crisis at home and strengthen their own power within Syria.

Syrian president Shukri al-Quwatli (left, in car) inspects his troops and a Czechoslovakian-made tank during a 1957 military parade in Damascus. Quwatli, a Ba'thist, fostered close ties to the Soviet Union and its allies.

Quwatli and Egyptian president Gamal Abdel Nasser wave to crowds in Cairo after the 1958 announcement that Syria and Egypt would unite as the United Arab Republic. Nasser, a socialist like Quwatli, was a hero throughout most of the Arab world for his forcefulness in promoting Arab interests.

A series of negotiations took place between Nasser, the Ba'th, and the military men linked to the Ba'th. On February 1, 1958, Nasser made a dramatic announcement: "Today Arab nationalism is not just a matter of slogans and shouts; it has become an actual reality, today the Arab people of Syria have united with the Arab people of Egypt to form the United Arab Republic." A referendum in the two countries approved the creation of the United Arab Republic (UAR) and Nasser was elected president of the union with an overwhelming majority.

Syrian expectations for this new political arrangement were quickly disappointed. Desperate to avoid further civil unrest, the Ba'th party and its military supporters agreed to all of Nasser's terms, many of which were harsh. Nasser demanded, among other things, that Syria's political parties be dissolved and that the Syrian army remove itself completely from political activity. In order to ensure compliance with this second condition, Nasser set out to bring the Syrian armed forces under his control. A number of Syrian officers were dismissed or transferred to Egypt. Among the second group was Hafez al-Assad.

Assad later spoke bitterly about his experiences under the UAR. He and other Syrian officers were placed under Egyptian military command. The jobs they were assigned were dull and unimportant. As Majid Khadduri put it: "It became clear that the services of Syrian officers were neither needed nor appreciated by their Egyptian superiors. Secret contacts with fellow officers at home indicated that their condition was not much better, and led them to believe that unity with Egypt could not last too long."

Assad and his fellow Syrians began to hold informal meetings. These led to the formation of a secret organization later known as the Ba'thist Military Committee. Five men were the prime forces behind the new group: Hafez al-Assad, Muhammad Umran, Salah Jadid, Abd al-Karim al-Jundi, and Ahmad al-Mir. All were connected with the Ba'th party and, significantly, all were Alawis.

During the next two years the Military Committee attracted a number of other Syrian officers. These included Alawis and officers from the large Druze minority. All of these men, Assad included, were growing increasingly critical of the older leadership of the Ba'th, particularly Aflaq and Bitar. The officers blamed them for giving in too easily to Nasser's demands.

By 1961 union with Egypt had become very unpopular in Syria. Nasser had adopted oppressive economic and political measures that alienated many Syrians. This was no less true for the Syrian leadership, both civilian and military. Civilian leaders, including officials of the Ba'th party, were fighting the ban on political organizations. In September 1961 a group of Syrian officers seized power in Damascus and demanded that Nasser agree to give Syria greater freedoms within the UAR. Nasser refused.

British planes patrol Egypt's Suez Canal in 1958. In 1956, after the United States and Britain halted aid to Nasser's socialist regime, Egypt seized the British-controlled canal, prompting Britain, France, and Israel to invade and retake it. Despite the defeat, Nasser was hailed by most Arabs for standing up to Western powers and Israel.

Within 24 hours the Syrian officers responded to the Egyptian leader's decision by announcing that Syria was withdrawing from the UAR. The political experiment, intended to foster Arab unity, had failed. Nasser would work furiously over the next months to force Syria back into the union, but his efforts would be in vain.

While these events were taking place, Assad and other officers from the Military Committee were stationed in the Suez Canal Zone in northern Egypt. Although they had played no part in the decision to withdraw from the union, Nasser ordered their arrest. They were accused of having plotted in secret against Egypt and the UAR.

Assad and the others returned to Syria after

nearly two months in an Egyptian military prison. No sooner had they set foot in Syria when they were humiliated once again. The new regime had struck against the Ba'thists after taking power. Many pro-Ba'th officers were dismissed from the military and given lowly jobs in the bureaucracy. Assad himself was given a desk job in the ministry of transportation.

Syria was again in turmoil. Many Syrians felt that their nation had been taken advantage of in the UAR, and the Ba'th party took much of the blame for the union agreement and for Nasser's repressive rule. The Ba'th itself was now divided into different rival factions and was politically very weak. The situation in Syria remained unstable for 18 months.

The new regime was headed by a group of conservative politicians and officers. They faced opposition from Egypt and from pro-Nasserite groups within Syria as well as other political forces, especially those on the left. It soon became clear the regime was incapable of uniting the country behind it.

The Military Committee had no intention of accepting this situation. The underground group continued its political activities and established a loose alliance with two other factions of officers opposed to the regime. One of these was a pro-Nasser group that favored union with Egypt, the other a faction

Syrian premier and Ba'th party cofounder Salah Bitar (right) in 1963. Syria, charging that Nasser was dominating the UAR, withdrew from the union in 1961 after an anti-Ba'thist coup. But in 1963 the Ba'thists regained power in another coup, and Assad was promoted to a top post in the air force.

of independent officers. The three organizations banded together to overthrow the government.

By early 1963 they were ready. On March 8 the alliance staged a bloodless coup that easily overthrew the weak and divided regime. The new government reinstated Assad and the rest of the Military Committee to their army posts. Although the alliance had only one group within it associated with the Ba'th, the coup became known as the Ba'thist Revolution of 1963. This was because only months after the takeover the Ba'thist officers joined with the Military Committee to force their allies out of power.

According to Itamar Rabinovitch, an Israeli historian, the Military Committee had held talks with Aflaq and Bitar before the coup. Although the officers distrusted the Ba'th leaders, they knew that an alliance with them would boost their own political power. Following the coup, links between the Military Committee and the party were made official.

The leaders of the Ba'th, now aligned with the Military Committee, set out to dominate the government. Their strongest opponent was the pro-Nasser group of officers. Friction between the Nasserites and the Ba'thists had developed only days after the coup. As the rivalry between the two groups intensified, the Ba'thists slowly gained the upper hand. The Military Committee purged the army of a large group of Nasserites in April 1963. At the same time they arrested a number of pro-Nasser civilian leaders.

By the summer of 1963 the Nasserite officers could sense defeat. In a last-ditch effort they attempted a coup in Damascus. Violence erupted. The pro-Nasser group was finally crushed after hours of fighting in which approximately 800 people — mostly civilians — were killed. The Ba'th was now in control of the Syrian state. The man who headed the new regime was Amin al-Hafez, a Sunni officer from Aleppo.

Although he hoped to govern a more stable, progressive Syria, in reality Hafez would preside over yet another period of national upheaval. Two large divisions had appeared in Syrian politics. One was led by Aflaq, Bitar, and other older Ba'thist leaders. They were moderates who continued to embrace the idea of Arab unity. The other division was dubbed the Regionalists because it was headed by men more concerned with the "region" of Syria than with the greater Arab world. The Regionalists were mostly younger and more radical men. Assad and the rest of the Military Committee broke with Aflaq and Bitar and threw their support behind the Regionalist faction.

The Military Committee set out to establish control over the armed forces. Assad and some of his allies assumed key positions within the army and

Syrian president Amin al-Hafez in 1963. Assad supported Hafez against the faction led by Bitar, and Hafez rewarded Assad in 1964 by promoting him to major general and giving him command of the air force.

Major General Salah Jadid, leader of the 1966 overthrow of the Hafez government, the 13th coup in Syria's 17 years of independence. Assad's refusal to bring the air force to the aid of Hafez was critical to Jadid's victory and helped establish Assad as one of the most powerful men in Syria.

air force. Assad, after being promoted first to major and then to lieutenant colonel, rose to a top position in the air force.

Assad's star continued to rise. In 1964 he was again promoted, this time to major general. He now became the official commander of the air force. Typically, he took advantage of his position to advance himself politically. He appointed close associates to key positions in the air force and set up a new intelligence network that served as his personal information service. In this way he could keep track of Syria's shifting political scene — and the plans and ambitions of allies and foes alike.

To consolidate their power, Military Committee members purged the Syrian army and air force of officers not aligned with them. The ousted soldiers, most of whom were Sunnis, were replaced with Alawi and Druze officers. These measures were opposed by the Sunni community, which was becoming deeply resentful of the Ba'thist regime and the rising Alawi domination of the state. Many Sunnis accused Assad and the other members of the committee of discrimination and nepotism. It would not be the last time Assad would hear these charges.

The Military Committee's strong-arm tactics not only fueled the resentment of the Sunni majority but also left the Ba'th government deeply divided and therefore less able to cope with pressing social and economic problems. Different factions in the state and the military struggled to assert themselves. In 1965 one long-standing rivalry in the military finally brought the government down.

The adversaries were Amin al-Hafez, the president of Syria's ruling Revolutionary Council, and Salah Jadid, a top officer and Military Committee member. Hafez's main support was within the Ba'th party; Jadid was strongest within the military. As the rivalry grew more intense, two large coalitions emerged in the top circles of power. Jadid's position was strengthened when many of Hafez's supporters in the officer corps went over to Jadid. In February 1966 the conflict erupted in violence.

Jadid's forces rose up in the Syrian capital and across the nation to stage the bloodiest of the 13 coups that the troubled nation had seen in 17 years. In Damascus, Hafez and a small group of supporters fought against Jadid's allies but were eventually defeated. A wounded Hafez was arrested along with Bitar and other top Ba'thist leaders. Aflaq went underground and soon fled the country.

Assad played a key role in the coup. Until the end of 1965 he had sided with Hafez. Realizing that Jadid had the upper hand, however, he switched his allegiance to Jadid once the coup began. In doing so he deprived Hafez of the important support of the air force.

Assad's choice decided the outcome of the coup. Jadid rewarded Assad by appointing him minister of defense. His new post, coupled with his position as commander of the air force, made him the second most powerful figure in Syrian politics. Only Salah Jadid stood between him and control of Syria.

> *Matters came to a head with yet another coup, the thirteenth and bloodiest in 17 years. It succeeded because the strong man, Hafez al-Assad, saw his chance and deserted Amin al-Hafez to support the coup.*
> —DEREK HOPWOOD
> professor of Middle
> Eastern history

5

"Demands and Aspirations"

Assad's alliance with Jadid lasted only a short while. After the two men succeeded in overthrowing Amin al-Hafez and the older leadership of the Ba'th, their cooperation gave way to an intense rivalry. Assad already had the support of the air force, and, as minister of defense, he was now able to begin building a power base in the army as well. As he had done earlier in the air force, he promoted his allies in the army — many of them Alawis — to important positions. The government and the military quickly split into two large factions, one backing Jadid, the other Assad.

Assad and Jadid's rivalry was based on warring ambitions, but the conflict between the two men also arose from their different approaches to the problems facing Syria. In the area of domestic policy the main issues were economic. Jadid set out to establish a set of radical socialist policies that would affect the entire economy. He proposed, for example,

> *No Palestinian should suffer the illusion that Palestine could be freed without the participation of Syria.*
> —MUSTAFA TLAS
> Syrian chief of staff

Assad in 1967, as minister of defense in the Jadid government. Assad and Jadid quickly developed a bitter rivalry: Their struggle for power was finally decided in favor of Assad, who had the support of powerful members of the air force and army.

Palestinian refugees fleeing their homes in Palestine during the 1948 war. The Palestine Liberation Organization (PLO) was founded in May 1964. This political and military group dedicated itself to defeating Israel and restoring Palestine to Palestinian Arabs.

that the state nationalize large areas of agriculture and industry. The state, he felt, should control production and economic development. Assad's approach to the economy was more moderate. He argued against sweeping measures, saying that nationalization on a grand scale would hurt the economy and increase domestic and international opposition to the regime. Free enterprise, he maintained, should be allowed to play a part in Syria's economic development.

The sharpest disagreements between the two men arose in the area of foreign policy. While Assad supported a flexible, pragmatic approach to international affairs, the Jadid government took a more radical position. Jadid's criticisms of moderate Arab rulers, including those of Saudi Arabia, Leb-

anon, and Jordan, led to an increasing isolation of Syria. Commercial and political links with these other countries dissolved, damaging both Syria's economy and its image. Jadid had an especially antagonistic relationship with King Hussein of Jordan. He accused Hussein of being too conciliatory toward Israel — a major offense in the eyes of hardline Arab nationalists.

Despite their differences, Jadid and Assad shared a common problem: Both were widely resented by those they governed. Their power struggles were fought out in the top circles of the state and within the Ba'th party, while the great majority of Syrians had little or no say in their government. This powerlessness fed the anger of many Syrians toward both leaders.

Sectarian rivalries were at the heart of these feelings. In one way or another, Sunnis and Alawis had been at odds for centuries, and the new political situation fueled this antagonism. Assad and Jadid were both Alawis, as were many of their top supporters in the Ba'th and the military. Alawi influence over Syrian politics was growing rapidly. The nation's Sunni majority felt increasingly alienated from the government.

Other events in 1966 only exacerbated the sectarian problem. In September a Druze general, Salim Hatum, staged a coup against the new regime. The revolt failed and the regime purged the army of many Druze officers. In most cases, these soldiers were replaced by Alawis loyal to Jadid or Assad. These actions only helped convince the Sunnis, as well as the Druze, that the Ba'thist government was determined to keep all non-Alawis out of the political process.

Jadid and Assad had to contend with enemies abroad as well as at home. Both men felt that the nation of Israel had unjustly deprived the Palestinians of their homeland and posed a threat to Syria and the rest of the Middle East. This hostility had begun with the creation of Israel in 1948 and had been fueled by certain policies adopted by Israel in the 1950s. Especially galling to the Syrians was the Israeli government's decision to divert the waters of the Jordan River.

The Israeli plan was to use the diverted river water to irrigate southern Israel's deserts. However, the Jordan was recognized as an international river whose waters were to be shared by all the countries bordering on it. The Israeli diversion was a clear violation of this status. Syria argued that Israel was not only threatening to take over the waterway but that it was also seizing Arab-owned lands along the river. Israel denied the Syrian claims, and by 1964 the Israeli project was completed and began operation. The diversion project increased tensions between Israel and the Arab states throughout the 1960s. At several points warfare seemed imminent. Israeli attacks on Syria and Egypt throughout this period only hardened positions on both sides.

Yasir Arafat in 1985. Arafat emerged in the 1960s as the leader of al-Fatah, a Palestinian guerrilla group. Al-Fatah was then supported by Syria, which sought to displace Nasser's Egypt as the leading nation of the pan-Arabist movement. Arafat eventually became chairman of the PLO.

In May 1964 new opposition against Israel arose with the creation of the Palestine Liberation Organization (PLO) and the Palestine Liberation Army (PLA). These groups were established by Palestinians with the aim of carrying out an armed struggle to liberate their occupied homeland. At the same time another Palestinian organization was growing increasingly active. This was the al-Fatah group headed by Yasir Arafat. In January 1965, Fatah launched a series of raids against Israel. These attacks were minor in military terms, but they created an enormous political stir.

The Israelis responded to the raids with a series of air and land attacks. Because most of the guerrilla raids had been launched from Jordan, that country became Israel's principal target. The main aim of these attacks was to put pressure on the Arab states to withdraw their support of the Palestinian guerrillas.

In practical terms Israel was striking against the wrong target. Most of the political and material support to the guerrillas had come from Syria, not Jordan. The Ba'thist government in Damascus supported the Palestinians for two reasons: First, it gave meaning to the Ba'thist call for Arab unity and activity against Israel; second, the Syrians hoped to challenge Nasser's position in the Arab world by taking the lead in the fight against Israel.

Syrian support for the guerrillas only increased in 1966 when Jadid seized power. One reason for this was historical. Many Syrians, Jadid included, felt that Palestine was historically a part of Syria that the French had taken away during the mandate. Jadid also gave support to the Palestinian cause because it fit very well with his radical stance against the Jewish state. During his years in power, he provided the Palestinians with a great deal of political and material support.

Assad generally supported Jadid's stance on Israel, but like his positions on other issues, Assad's approach was more measured and pragmatic. Because Jadid distrusted the heads of the other Arab states, he felt that Syria should bear the responsibility of supporting a Palestinian uprising. Assad

> *The Palestinian tragedy . . . has, unlike most great upheavals in history, a specific starting point: the year 1897. In this year . . . the World Zionist Organization . . . resolved in its programme to work towards the establishment of a Jewish state on Arab soil.*
>
> —WALID KHALIDI
> Palestinian historian

felt that all Arab nations should band together to fight Israel. In this way, Arab strength would be increased — and Syria would not be the only Middle Eastern nation to face possible reprisals by Israel's powerful military. Assad summed up his position late in the 1960s when he spoke before a Ba'th party congress: "I have repeatedly stressed the importance of Arab military coordination — notably among the Arab states that border with Israel — regardless of the differences and the contradictions in their political positions, as long as it would serve the armed struggle."

On June 5, 1967, Assad's vision of a united Arab front against Israel became a reality as Syria joined Jordan and Egypt in a war against Israel. Although the Arabs had been confident that their combined forces could crush the small Jewish state, the Israelis triumphed in the conflict, which lasted only one week. Syrian losses in the war included much of its air force and the territory known as the Golan Heights. Perhaps just as serious for the Syrian regime was the loss of prestige. Already alienated from much of the population, the government now faced a new wave of criticism and opposition from nearly every sector of Syrian society.

Syrians march through the streets of Damascus in October 1966 in support of the Palestinian cause. Support for the Palestinians and opposition to Israel was widespread throughout Syria, the other Arab nations, and most of the Muslim world.

A group of Palestinians views the wreckage of their homes in a Jordanian village after an Israeli air raid in the mid-1960s. In 1965, the Israeli government began bombing Jordanian villages, refugee camps, and Palestinian military bases in response, it said, to al-Fatah and PLO guerrilla attacks.

The sharpest criticism was leveled at the nation's military, which had been quickly vanquished by the Israeli army. Many of the charges were aimed specifically at Assad himself. As minister of defense, he was held accountable for the armed forces' poor performance. Some critics, for example, blamed him for the loss of the Golan Heights.

Not only was Assad accused of military incompetence, he was charged with betraying his country by approving a misleading radio broadcast that contributed to the loss of the Golan Heights. Five days after the start of the war Radio Damascus reported that Quneitra, the provincial capital of the Golan Heights, had fallen to the Israelis. This announcement was made, however, hours before the first Israeli soldier even approached the town. Upon hearing the broadcast, Syrian troops panicked and

quickly retreated, leaving the town nearly de-
fenseless.

The radio report had been authorized by the ministry of defense, which means that Assad must have
known about it. Some Syrians saw this as evidence
that their defense minister was working with the
Israelis. But these charges seem unlikely, especially
in light of Assad's later record of strident opposition
to the Jewish state. Other analysts have suggested
a more likely explanation for the broadcast: The
ministry hoped that the announcement would
prompt UN officials to impose a cease-fire on Israel
before the important city had fallen. But this, unfortunately for Syria, did not happen. Instead, the
Israelis entered Quneitra unopposed and established control there before the cease-fire went into
effect that evening.

Assad was also charged with putting his personal priorities above those of his nation. Many observers felt the Syrians had displayed little skill or organization in the 1967 fighting. Some Syrians argued that the reason for this was that Assad and the regime had pulled the best troops off the front lines before the fighting began. These troops, many of them Alawis, were kept in Damascus, where they were used to defend the regime in the case of an uprising.

Although Syria's government was badly shaken by the military defeat and the renewed opposition within Syria, the regime managed to stay in power. However, the defeat added new fuel to the rivalry between Assad and Jadid as Assad began to rethink his military and strategic policies. Prior to the war, Assad had voiced little opposition to Jadid's aggressive stance against Israel and his call for a Syrian-backed "people's struggle" to defeat the Jewish state. But in light of Syria's poor performance in the 1967 war, Assad now modified his views. He and his supporters now insisted that the govern-

An Israeli soldier guards a checkpoint in Israeli-held territory near the Syrian town of Quneitra during the 1967 Six-Day War. Israel won the war, taking the Golan Heights from Syria, the Sinai Peninsula from Egypt, and the West Bank region from Jordan.

ment should stop promoting resistance to Israel until it had improved its armed forces. This, they said, should take place even before further economic development. Jadid and his faction disagreed. They felt military buildup and economic projects could both be carried out without any threat to Syria's strength.

Assad's opposition to Jadid's domestic policies also heightened during this period. Assad and his followers called for a more practical and moderate approach to political matters. Syria, they said, needed to strengthen its political position after the disastrous war. This meant building better relations with the other Arab states. It also meant a less repressive policy within Syria. Assad urged government officials to cooperate with other political forces within the country and to bring them into the decision-making process.

Assad's ideas were rejected by the Jadid regime. Sensing the impending showdown with Jadid, Assad continued to take measures to build up his position. He promoted more of his supporters to key

positions. He also gave support to officers who had clashed with Jadid's faction. By now the country was being ruled by two governments — a civilian body headed by Jadid and a military regime headed by Assad.

In February 1969, Assad tried to bring this impossible situation to an end by seizing power. He mobilized his troops, took over newspaper offices and the national radio station, and arrested a number of his opponents. But his attempted coup was only partly successful. Jadid was still strong enough within the Ba'th and the military to withstand Assad's challenge. The result was that Syria's two governments continued to exist. The partial coup did enable Assad and his supporters to have more input into policy decisions, but the basic conflict between the two men remained.

In September 1970—a month known to some Palestinians as Black September—the rivalry escalated to new heights. Again, the issue was support for the Palestinians, this time in Jordan. King Hussein had already clashed several times with Jordan's large, politically influential Palestinian community, which he saw as a challenge to his own rule. In September a full military conflict erupted as Hussein sent his army in to crush the Palestinian organizations.

The Syrian regime decided to assist the Palestinians. A Syrian-backed force of the PLA was sent in. After initial successes against Jordan's army, Syrian and Palestinian troops were forced to withdraw and suffered heavy casualties during their retreat. As in 1967, questions were raised about Assad's role in this unsuccessful conflict. He seems to have approved a limited action, but he refused to provide air force support for the Syrian-backed troops. Assad's reasons for this decision are not clear, although he may have been trying to embarrass the Jadid government.

This episode sparked the final struggle between Assad and Jadid. The Jadid faction struck first. At a Ba'th party congress held in early November the Ba'th membership voted to oust Assad and his top general, Mustafa Tlas. Assad wasted no time in responding: On November 13, 1970, he ordered his troops to occupy Ba'th headquarters and to arrest the leaders of the regime and any officers who still supported Jadid. Some top members of the government managed to flee the country. Jadid and others were arrested and imprisoned.

Hafez al-Assad was now firmly in control. He never referred to his takeover as a revolution. Instead he termed it a "corrective movement" that had come about "in response to our people's demands and aspirations." Assad and his supporters claimed that they had not overthrown a legitimate government but merely a small group of radicals. And, with their removal, Syria and the Ba'th could return to the important work of uniting the country and improving its prestige in the international community. As Assad would discover, this would be no easy task.

> *Assad's primary task in taking over in 1970 was to establish some stability in the regime.*
> —DEREK HOPWOOD
> professor of Middle
> Eastern history

6

Arab Champion

In consolidating his newly won position as Syria's leader, Hafez al-Assad faced two different but related tasks. The first was to strengthen his support among those groups that already backed him. Assad wanted to ensure that in periods of trouble he had a firm power base to depend on. The other, more difficult task was to establish better relations with those groups that opposed him.

The armed forces were Assad's main source of support. Since 1963 the military had been closely involved in Syrian politics. Aware of its growing power, Syrian leaders gave special treatment to the military in order to win its loyalty. By 1970 the officer corps in particular was a privileged group that enjoyed a number of special benefits, such as high salaries, excellent housing, and free medical care.

Assad did nothing to change this system. He had, after all, benefited from it himself. The high salaries and all the other privileges remained. Beginning in 1970, Assad went further. He made a point of paying close attention to the demands of the armed forces.

From the moment he seized power, Assad consciously tried to rule not only in the name of the Ba'th party, but as a leader of the country as a whole who would put all national organizations, including his own party, at the service of the nation.
—MAJID KHADDURI
professor of
political science

Assad as president of Syria, in July 1971. From the start of his regime, Assad sought to make Syria a major power in the Middle East. By the 1980s he had succeeded in that aim.

After taking power in 1970, Assad began to reach out to other political factions in order to broaden his support. As Majid Khadduri noted, the Syrian president saw this as a way to end the isolation of the Ba'thist regime: "He realized that before the Ba'th party could claim popular support, cooperation with other groups was necessary before the principles of Arab unity, freedom, and socialism were fully accepted."

Accordingly, Assad formed an alliance that came to be known as the National Progressive Front. This coalition encompassed the Ba'th party and several other groups, including the Syrian Communist party. These smaller parties were given seats in the People's Council — the first Syrian legislative body to convene since 1966. They had little actual political power, but Assad did give them recognition and a small voice in governmental decision making. In this way Assad accomplished two goals: He retained virtually absolute control over Syrian policy and broadened his support by placating his political opponents.

Arab heads of state sign an agreement establishing the Federation of Arab Republics, a short-lived pan-Arabist confederation. Seated from right to left are Assad, Libyan premier Muammar el-Qaddafi, and Egyptian president Anwar Sadat, who succeeded to the office upon the death of Nasser in 1970.

As a canny politician, Assad was well aware that he must appease Syria's Sunni majority, his largest opposition group. To achieve this goal, Assad took a series of measures, many of which were purely symbolic. In the words of Moshe Ma'oz: "Assad presented himself as a devout Muslim, to be sure, and hailed the role of Islam in national life. He participated in public prayers and religious ceremonies . . . encouraged the construction of new mosques, raised the salaries of many religious functionaries, and appointed a Sunni as minister of religious endowments." Assad also appointed Sunnis to top positions in his government. During the 1970s and 1980s Sunnis would serve in the posts of foreign minister, prime minister, and even defense minister.

But Assad was only partly successful in winning the support of the Sunni community. Sunni opposition grew less active for a few years after the 1970 coup. By the end of the decade, however, it would return with new fury. The Muslim Brotherhood, the group that staged the 1982 coup in Hama, played a leading role in organizing this renewed opposition.

The body of a Syrian soldier lies beside a disabled tank on the Golan Heights during the October War of 1973 (also called the Yom Kippur War) between Israel and its Arab neighbors. Syria failed to retake the territory it had lost in the Six-Day War of 1967, but Assad emerged from the war more popular than ever among the Syrian public.

Assad confers with his brother Rifat al-Assad during a 1974 visit to a military installation on the Syrian side of the Golan Heights. Rifat led the Defense Companies, the crack military unit charged with suppressing domestic opposition to the Assad regime.

Internal dissent was not Assad's only worry as he established his government, however; international rivalries were also a primary concern of the fledgling regime. Under Jadid, Syria's political isolation had increased. Relations with the other Arab nations were at a new low when Assad took power.

President Assad showed considerable skill in mending these relations. In the first three years of his rule he traveled frequently to other Arab capitals, meeting with fellow leaders. He improved Syria's ties with several Middle Eastern nations, including Egypt, Jordan, Saudi Arabia, and Lebanon. In 1971, Assad joined with Egypt and Libya to create a loose political association known as the Federation of Arab Republics (FAR). Although the FAR never amounted to very much, Assad demonstrated his commitment to Arab unity and cooperation simply by joining the federation. Assad also signed a military pact with Egypt around the same time.

Assad's approach to the Palestinian movement reflected his primary foreign policy goals — promoting Arab unity and undermining the state of Israel. Because he sought to achieve these ends in a pragmatic manner, he adopted a supportive yet ambiguous policy toward the Palestinian nationalists. Assad continued Jadid's policy of providing strong military and financial support to the guerrillas. Since the Palestinian cause was very popular in Syria, these policies also increased his domestic support.

But Assad was aware of the potential threat posed by a large and well-armed guerrilla movement. He had seen Hussein of Jordan send troops against the guerrillas in 1970 because he had felt the rebels were challenging his regime. Accordingly, Assad repeatedly asserted his authority over Syria's Palestinian community. In 1970 he cracked down on a Palestinian organization known as al-Sa'iqah, which had been established by Jadid in the early 1960s. Al-Sa'iqah now fell under Assad's authority.

By 1973, Assad's efforts at consolidating his power at home and abroad were paying off. He had acquired respect and support from many groups within Syria. He had also come to be known as a statesman within the Arab world. His political position was now stronger than that of any Syrian leader before him.

With this new stature Assad was ready to focus his energies on the still unresolved struggle with Israel. Tensions between Israel and the Arab states had only grown worse since the 1967 war. Jordan, Syria, and Egypt had all lost land to Israel in that conflict. Arab frustration mounted as Israel continued to occupy these territories.

As they had in 1948 and 1967, the Arab nations once again decided to join forces against Israel. Assad and Anwar Sadat, the Egyptian president who took over after Nasser died in 1970, had already

Former Israeli prisoners of war return from Syria to Tel Aviv, Israel, after being exchanged for Syrian, Moroccan, and Iraqi prisoners in 1974. After the October War, Assad turned his attention to building Syria's economy.

signed a military accord. In a series of talks that also involved representatives from Jordan, Morocco, Iraq, Saudi Arabia, and Kuwait, the Arab leaders quietly drew up plans for a concerted attack on Israel. All the nations pledged to send military forces into battle, and the oil-producing states agreed to an embargo that would put pressure on Israel's allies in Europe and on the United States. The offensive was launched on October 6, 1973, which happened to be both Assad's 43rd birthday and Yom Kippur, the holiest day in the Jewish calendar. Assad's long-cherished vision of the Arab Middle East rising up against Israel seemed to be taking shape.

The Arab armies scored early successes. Israel had been taken by surprise, and its forces were put on the defensive. By the second week of fighting, however, Israel began to turn the tide. One very important factor in this resistance was a series of arms shipments by the United States, which gave Israel a military advantage.

A cease-fire was declared on October 22 following intense diplomatic activity by the American secretary of state, Henry Kissinger, and representatives from Israel, Syria, and Egypt. Sadat accepted the cease-fire eagerly; Assad did so reluctantly. He would later charge that Egypt, Syria's strongest ally in the Yom Kippur War, had only entered the conflict to force negotiations so that it could recover the territory it had lost in the 1967 war. Sadat, Assad asserted, had little interest in an all-out war against Israel or in helping Syria recover the Golan Heights, which had also been occupied by Israel in 1967.

Despite the final defeat and the heavy losses suffered by the Syrian army and air force, Assad came out of the war more popular than ever. His army had fought well, and although they had been stopped, Assad felt that their initial successes had shown that Israel was not invulnerable. And, in tough negotiations with Kissinger after the cease-fire, Assad showed himself to be a shrewd and stubborn diplomat. In his memoirs, Kissinger remarked that Assad negotiated "daringly and tenaciously like a riverboat gambler to make sure that he had exacted the last sliver of available concessions."

We say now as we have always said—that peace should be based on complete withdrawal [of Israel] from the lands occupied in 1967 and on the full restoration of the rights of the Palestinian people.
—HAFEZ AL-ASSAD
in a 1975 speech

As Assad's popularity rose, some political observers began to consider him the preeminent leader of the Arab world. Many people now compared him with Gamal Abdel Nasser, a comparison that Assad actively encouraged. In speeches he made frequent mention of Nasser and often had his own portrait displayed alongside that of the late Egyptian leader.

By 1974, Assad was at the peak of his power and influence. He was not only the head of both the armed forces and the government but now had control over all domestic and foreign policy as well. Firmly in power, Assad was able to concentrate on the economic and political development of Syria, which was experiencing a period of stability and relative prosperity. But this tranquil time would only last a few short years.

In neighboring Lebanon political unrest was escalating toward armed conflict. As Assad turned his attention to the Lebanese crisis, a new wave of opposition within Syria would begin to emerge. Both developments were soon to push Syria into a new era of turmoil and bloodshed. For Hafez al-Assad, it was to be the most challenging and frustrating period of his political life.

Assad and U.S. secretary of state Henry Kissinger confer in Damascus during the peace negotiations that followed the Yom Kippur War. Kissinger later praised Assad as a "daring and tenacious" negotiator.

7

Trouble at Home and Abroad

The Republic of Lebanon was founded in 1946, the same year that Syria achieved its independence. At the time Lebanon gained its independence the two largest religious communities in Lebanon were the Sunni Muslims and the Maronites, a Christian sect. During the decades that followed, the nation's population figures shifted as other groups, particularly Shi'ite Muslims, grew in numbers.

Lebanon's political system was fragile from the start. The national government was based on a distribution of power whereby each religious community was given a fixed share of the top positions in the government and a certain number of seats in the parliament. The two largest groups, the Maronites and the Sunnis, received most of the political power, with the Maronites dominating slightly. For a short time, into the 1950s, this system worked fairly well.

Throughout history Syria and Lebanon have been one country and people.
—HAFEZ AL-ASSAD

A Palestinian refugee camp in Beirut, Lebanon, in the early 1970s. When Jordan expelled the Palestinians after heavy fighting in 1970, many of the refugees moved to Lebanon, joining the large number of Palestinians already living in the small nation situated between Israel and Syria.

A Palestinian refugee camp near the southern Lebanese city of Tripoli in the 1950s. Formerly part of Syria, Lebanon was granted its independence from the French in 1946. The delicate balance of power between Lebanon's Christians and Muslims was upset by the influx of large numbers of Palestinians.

By the late 1950s, however, mounting social and economic problems began to put a strain on Lebanon's political system. As in Syria's early years of independence, political power in Lebanon was dominated by a small group of traditional leaders, most of whom were Maronites or Sunni Muslims. Also as in Syria, these leaders were usually unable or unwilling to work together to find solutions to the problems confonting Lebanon. As a result they began to face challenges from younger, more dynamic leaders, many of whom were calling for substantial changes in Lebanon's political and economic policies.

Fuel was added to this political fire by the presence of the Palestinians in Lebanon. Since the creation of the state of Israel in 1948, large numbers of Palestinian refugees had settled in Lebanon. By the late 1960s, refugee camps had become centers

of recruitment and activity by Yasir Arafat's al-Fatah and other guerrilla organizations. The rebels used Lebanon as a base for their raids on Israel, especially after the PLO was driven out of Jordan in 1970. Israel responded with fierce attacks, which were often aimed at the Lebanese and Palestinian civilian population. Fearful of the well-armed guerrillas and frustrated with Israel's attacks, Maronite and other Lebanese leaders began to insist that the Palestinians leave the country.

These problems came to a head in 1974 and 1975. Violent incidents led to full-scale battles between militias of the Maronite community and a coalition of leftist and Muslim groups, which had long resented their secondary status. The Lebanese civil war had started. At first the Palestinians stayed out of the conflict. Then, in early 1976, the PLO joined the coalition of forces fighting the Maronites.

Assad viewed the turmoil in Lebanon with growing concern. On several occasions in 1975 and early 1976 he sent envoys to Lebanon to help negotiate an end to the violence. These attempts failed and the fighting continued. After putting new pressures on the Lebanese leadership and achieving few results, Assad decided to send in his army to force an end to the conflict.

Assad had several reasons for intervening in Lebanon. The first was shared by many Syrians. Like them, Assad viewed Lebanon as a historical part of Syria. The French, he felt, had arbitrarily separated Lebanon from Syria during the mandate period. "Throughout history," he argued, "Syria and Lebanon have been one country and one people." He therefore maintained that Syria had a right to become involved in Lebanese affairs.

From the Arab nationalist point of view, it was not permissible to accord the French-created Lebanese republic recognition as a nation-state separate and distinct from Syria.

—KAMAL SALIBI
Lebanese historian

Another factor influenced Assad as well. He feared that if the leftist Palestinian coalition achieved a full victory in Lebanon they would establish a new and radical state. Assad was determined to prevent this from happening. Such a radical state on his border, he felt, would work with Syrian opposition groups to challenge his regime.

Assad was also motivated by a desire to control the activities of the Palestinian guerrillas. Although he supported their struggle against Israel, he wanted to have the final say on how and when this struggle would be conducted. He argued that Syria and the other Arab states could only fight Israel when they were prepared. Assad was afraid that the guerrillas, through their raids, would draw Syria into war at the wrong time. For this reason he worked to keep them under his control.

By May 1976 the Palestinians and their leftist-Muslim allies, known now as the Lebanese National Movement (LNM), had won a series of battles. The Maronites were on the defensive. Several months earlier Assad had extended his support to the Maronite leadership, including sending Syrian troops into Lebanon to fight against the LNM. He now decided on massive intervention. In late May and early June, thousands of Syrian troops moved into Lebanon. Although they were successfully resisted in several areas, they were able to prevent the LNM from overrunning the Maronite forces.

Sporadic fighting continued in Lebanon as the political situation continued to become increasingly complex. Finding a solution that both Assad and the Lebanese could accept was going to be extremely difficult. The Syrian president was aware of this fact early on. Although a solution seemed far off, he was nonetheless determined to stay in Lebanon and to play a key role in reaching a settlement.

The Maronite-Syrian alliance had been shaky from the start. Christian leaders were suspicious of Assad's intentions in Lebanon, and they were reluctant to work too closely with the head of a Muslim state. Assad, in turn, was no less suspicious of the Maronites. Within a year of the Syrian intervention the alliance fell apart. Assad's troops switched sides and engaged in violent battles against their former allies. Similar changes of allegiance would take place several times over the years as Syria struggled to keep up with Lebanon's changing political rivalries.

A Syrian tank crew keeps watch over Palestinian positions in Bhamdoun, Lebanon, during the Lebanese civil war in 1976. Israeli raids against the PLO, coupled with Lebanese Christian resentment against Palestinian Muslims, helped to ignite the civil war. Syrian forces moved into Lebanon in 1976 to bring a halt to the conflict.

The Lebanese conflict was further complicated by the actions of other Middle Eastern countries. Israel launched attacks on Palestinian and leftist positions in the south while providing arms and other supplies to the Maronite militias. In 1977, Israel's longtime enemy, Egypt, made a decision that would have an impact not only on Lebanon but on the entire region. After a long series of negotiations, President Anwar Sadat decided to end the conflict between his country and Israel. This not only shocked and outraged other Arab rulers, it encouraged both the Israelis and the Maronites in their war against the Palestinians in Lebanon.

As the battles raged on, confrontation between Syria and Israel seemed more and more likely. In March 1978, Israel launched a limited but furious invasion of southern Lebanon. This raised tensions even higher, which, in turn, led to more fighting between Syrian and Maronite forces. Assad's political difficulties abroad were now greater than ever.

President Assad also faced problems at home as unrest within Syria spread rapidly. Sunni resentment of the Ba'th party and its leaders had risen steadily despite Assad's attempts to appease the Sunni community by appointing members of their ranks to top political positions. Many realized that despite their titles, these individuals were figureheads, whereas Alawi officials remained the nation's real power brokers.

The Syrian government drew criticism not only because it was controlled by the Alawi minority but because it was becoming increasingly corrupt. During the 1970s members of the government grew steadily more involved in graft, smuggling, and other illegal practices. The president's brother Rifat al-Assad was believed to be at the center of these activities.

In 1976 and 1977 the popularity of Assad's regime plummeted. For many Syrians the intervention in Lebanon had been the last straw. Not only had the government stepped in to defend a group of conservative Christians, it was doing so to the detriment of the Lebanese Muslims and their Palestinian allies.

All of these grievances led to conflict between Syria's government and its citizens. Many different sectors of the society now actively opposed Assad. These included students, workers, professional groups, and the Sunni community as a whole.

Few of these groups had the strength to pose a serious threat to the regime. The president's internal security units were well organized and well armed. Assad had carefully built up these organizations and he used them effectively. One group, however, did emerge to challenge the government through active, and often violent, resistance. This was the Muslim Brotherhood.

The Muslim Brotherhood first emerged in Syria in the 1930s. Its doctrine that Arab nations should be governed by traditional Islamic teachings appealed to many, especially in the Sunni community.

An Israeli soldier guards two blindfolded Palestinian detainees along the Lebanon-Israel border in the mid-1970s. Al-Fatah and other Palestinian guerrilla groups, some under the sponsorship of the PLO, staged hit-and-run raids into Israel from Lebanese bases both before and after the outbreak of the civil war.

In the early 1960s the Brotherhood became a leading voice of opposition to the secular ideology of the Ba'th. Like his political predecessors, Assad faced the opposition of this group. The Muslim Brotherhood had broken up into different factions by this time, each with its own ideas on how to challenge the regime. Younger, more militant members argued that change could only come through armed struggle. This radical faction was especially strong in the northern Syrian cities of Aleppo, Hama, and Homs.

Brotherhood militants began their campaign of violence not long after the Syrian intervention in Lebanon began in 1976. Rebels carried out a series of assassinations of leading Alawis including military leaders, government officials, and civilians linked to the regime. Several members of Assad's family were among the Brotherhood's victims. Assassinations as well as bombings continued for the next few years.

One particularly grim event occurred in Aleppo in June 1979 when Brotherhood rebels gunned down 60 cadets at the local artillery school. Later that year the city was the scene of antigovernment riots and demonstrations. Local merchants declared a general strike, which spread to other towns. In response, the president sent in a large number of troops under the command of his brother Rifat al-Assad in March 1980. Hundreds of rebels and noncombatants were killed in the fighting that ensued.

As the Muslim Brotherhood expanded the scope of its operations, Assad tried to quiet the opposition through conciliatory statements and limited reforms. These attempts failed, mostly because they did not address the rebels' fundamental grievances. The struggle between the Brotherhood and the government continued. Inspired by the Islamic militants, new opposition groups also rose up to challenge Assad's regime.

Assad's responses to the growing rebel movement became increasingly harsh. This new hard-line stance emerged after two professional groups, the Conference of Engineers and the Lawyers Union, organized protests against the government in 1979.

In the final analysis the day of the evil regime that rules Syria will pass. . . . To this end . . . we must increase our faith, deepen our commitment, and hold faster to God than to our personal possessions and individuality. Patience is everything.
—Islamic movement opposed to Assad's regime

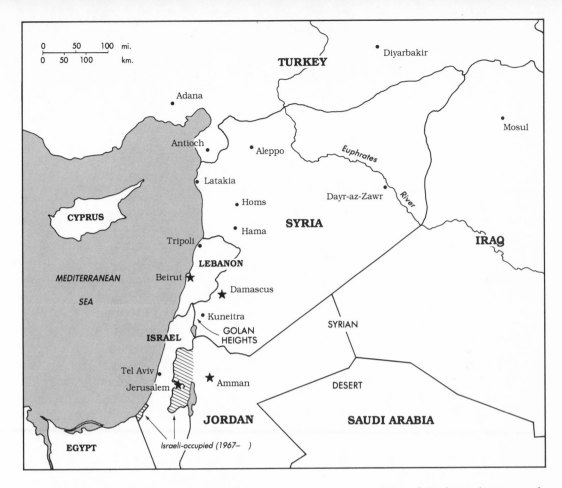

Map of Syria and surrounding territories. The shaded areas indicate the West Bank and Gaza Strip, occupied by Israel since 1967.

Assad dissolved both groups and had their leaders arrested. On June 26, 1980, the Muslim Brotherhood attempted to assassinate Assad himself. In retaliation, the regime struck back against the Brotherhood and other opposition groups with brutal measures, which included murdering hundreds of political prisoners. Several exiled critics of the regime were also killed. These included Salah Bitar, the cofounder of the Ba'th, who had charged that Assad had betrayed party ideals in the interest of retaining personal power.

Even these extreme measures did not quiet the opposition. Attacks against the state continued, especially in northern Syria. In August 1981 a bomb exploded in the office of the prime minister, killing 20 people. Assad's government was now in a state of war with the Brotherhood. This war claimed many casualties: Approximately 300 members of the regime were assassinated by dissidents, thou-

Assad (right) and his brother Rifat, who led government forces in crushing a Sunni uprising in Aleppo in 1980. After a failed attempt by the Muslim Brotherhood to kill Assad, Rifat led a crackdown that resulted in the death of thousands of opposition leaders, Brotherhood fighters, and civilians. The violence culminated in the repression of the Hama uprising.

sands of rebels were killed or jailed, and many civilians were caught in the crossfire. The climax of this conflict was the February 1982 Hama rebellion.

Assad's bloody suppression of the Hama revolt finally slowed the momentum of the opposition movement, though it did not end the opposition itself. Rebel forces regrouped and reconsidered strategies. The factions of the Muslim Brotherhood decided to forget their differences and join with other groups to work in unison against Assad and his government. This led to the formation of the National Alliance for the Liberation of Syria, which called for the immediate overthrow of the Assad regime.

According to British journalist and Assad biographer Patrick Seale, Assad's constant struggle to stay in power deflected him from his goals and corrupted his ideals. Although Seale, a longtime Mideast correspondent, had admired Assad, he changed his assessment in the early 1980s:

President Assad, the longest-serving ruler of independent Syria and an astute and reasonable man, now finds himself running a morally flawed regime practicing gangster methods indistinguishable from those of his adversaries. To meet terror, Assad has resorted to ferocious counter-terror, indiscriminate arrests, beating and torture, wholesale destruction of buildings thought to be sheltering suspects, reprisals against the families of the accused, shoot-outs and mass killings. . . . It is a sad come-down after the hopes and achievements of his early years.

The 1980s would be a challenging time for Hafez al-Assad. Dissent within Syria would flare up periodically, and international conflicts would force him to make many difficult decisions. But Assad was a man determined to stay in power — and to do all he could to shape the future of Syria and the entire Middle East.

8

The Ongoing Struggle

In his short biography of Assad published in 1981, Majid Khadduri presented a rare personal description of the Syrian leader. Assad, he wrote, "led a fairly austere private life and set an example of public service devoid of personal gain or self-indulgence in worldly affairs. He is married and has five children (four of them are boys), and his private life is essentially simple. He neither smokes nor drinks and he spends most of his time attending to public duties."

These public duties, in the 1980s, would give Assad little rest. By 1980, he was waging a difficult battle against a growing opposition movement. His regime, which had often been unpopular, was more alienated from the Syrian people than ever before. This domestic crisis came at a time when Syria was growing increasingly isolated from the rest of the Arab world.

> *While we see Arab nations all around us racing along the road to capitulation, Syria should double its efforts to prevent total Arab collapse.*
> —HAFEZ AL-ASSAD

Two Palestinian boys in Beirut display a portrait of Assad in 1982. Syrian military involvement in the Lebanon conflict was one reason for Syria's increasing isolation in the Arab world during the 1980s. By mid-decade only the radical Qaddafi regime of Libya was firmly allied with Syria.

This regional isolation was partly due to Assad's intervention in Lebanon. Syria's activities there had aroused the suspicions of other Arab leaders, many of whom were convinced that Assad sought to bring the troubled nation under his control. In an attempt to block Assad's plans, these leaders sent a new peacekeeping force to Lebanon. This group, known as the Arab Deterrent Force (ADF) and made up of troops from various Middle Eastern states, was established in October 1976 at an Arab summit meeting in Riyadh, Saudi Arabia. Most of these troops were Syrian, however, and, as a result, Assad retained control over the activities of the ADF.

Within Lebanon itself opposition to Assad's activities was growing. Many Lebanese had been against the Syrian intervention from the start. One particularly outspoken critic of Assad's policies was Kamal Jumblatt, the leader of the Lebanese Druze community. Jumblatt was assassinated shortly after he drove through a Syrian checkpoint on March 16, 1977. Many people, both inside and outside Lebanon, were convinced that the Assad regime was responsible for his death.

By 1980, relations with another Arab state, Egypt, were also very tense. Assad and Egyptian president Anwar Sadat had worked closely together in planning the 1973 war against Israel. But after Sadat signed a disengagement agreement with Israel in 1975, Assad angrily denounced Egypt's pact as a surrender to the Jewish state. Assad had always felt that a settlement with Israel could only come after the Arab states had achieved political unity. In his opinion, a just peace with Israel could only be achieved if the Arab nations joined together to pool their strength.

Because of this conviction, Assad was outraged when Sadat and the Israeli prime minister, Menachem Begin, signed the Camp David agreement in 1979. Calling the treaty a betrayal of the Arab cause, he severed all relations with Egypt. Sadat responded to Assad's criticism by denouncing the Syrian leader and charging that his regime was illegitimate. He termed Assad's government "the Alawi regime" and even referred to his supporters as "those dirty Alawis."

Assad's relations with King Hussein of Jordan were not much better. Tensions between Syria and Jordan had grown during the past few years. In 1979–80, Assad accused the Jordanians of providing arms and financial support to the Muslim Brotherhood. Hussein denied the charges and angrily criticized the Assad regime. Only later did Hussein indirectly confirm that his government had indeed supported the militants.

In late 1980, Assad mobilized a large Syrian force, complete with hundreds of tanks, on the Jordanian border. He warned that he would order his troops to cross into Jordan unless Hussein stopped aiding the Brotherhood. The crisis finally ended after envoys from Saudi Arabia met with Assad and Hussein. Tensions between the two regimes continued, however, into the 1980s.

That year, Assad also exchanged insults and accusations with the leaders of Iraq. The reasons for the disintegrating relations between Iraq and Syria were many and complicated. In 1979 the two countries had briefly worked together in opposing Sadat's peace initiative with Israel, but this short period of cooperation quickly collapsed. Among the reasons for the Syrian-Iraqi feud was that each nation accused the other of plotting against it by supporting local opposition movements. Alasdair Drysdale,

Assad watches as Soviet Communist party leader Leonid Brezhnev signs a Syrian-Soviet economic and political agreement in Moscow in 1974. Assad strengthened Syria's ties to the Soviet Union and made his country the superpower's closest ally in the Middle East.

An anti-U.S. demonstration in Damascus in 1983. The United States had accused Syria, along with Libya and Iran, of sponsoring terrorist attacks against American civilians and U.S. military and diplomatic officials.

the author of several articles on Syria, noted that these suspicions were probably correct, at least on Assad's part. "There are good grounds," Drysdale wrote, "to believe that many of the weapons finding their way into the hands of some Syrian opposition groups originate in Iraq." Relations between Syria and Iraq grew so hostile that when Iran and Iraq went to war in 1980, Syria backed Iran, a non-Arab nation. This decision earned Assad's government further condemnation from the other Arab states.

Despite its isolation, Syria did have one strong ally in the Middle East. In September 1980, Assad joined Libyan leader Muammar el-Qaddafi in announcing plans for a union between their two countries. For Assad this would be a beneficial arrangement because of Libya's oil wealth and because it would give Syria badly needed support in the Arab world. But perhaps because of Qaddafi's unpopularity in the international community, Assad postponed his nation's merger with Libya. The proposed union never took place, but the two rulers maintained good relations into the late 1980s.

Assad formed another, more important, alliance in 1980 when he signed a treaty of friendship and cooperation with the Soviet Union. Syrian ties to the Soviet Union went back to the mid-1950s, when the Soviets, interested in extending their influence in the Middle East, first offered Syria diplomatic support and large arms shipments. During the next three decades the relationship between the two countries remained cordial. The foundation of this alliance was a series of arms agreements. Between 1955 and 1980 the Soviets poured huge amounts of weapons into Syria.

Despite this assistance, the various regimes that governed Syria since the 1950s had shown great caution in dealing with the Soviet Union. Fearful of superpower domination, few Syrian politicians were anxious to put their country squarely in the Soviet camp. Also, Syria had commercial and political ties with Western states that a close relationship with Moscow might have put in jeopardy.

Nonetheless, on October 8, 1980, Assad signed a groundbreaking treaty that formalized ties with the Soviet Union. This decision was, in many ways, an indication of how isolated Assad felt at that point. For years Syria had refused Soviet offers for such a treaty. Assad's decision finally to sign came as he faced a growing number of domestic and regional pressures. Yet despite the new agreement, Assad would continue to pursue his own policies, some of which were criticized by the Soviets. These included his attempts to bring the Palestinian guerrilla movement under his control.

Assad's strengthened ties to the Soviet Union adversely affected his nation's relations with the United States. Even before the treaty, U.S.-Syrian relations had not been particularly strong. During Assad's rule they were often strained to the breaking point as the Syrian president repeatedly criticized the United States's Middle East policies. He voiced particular bitterness over the U.S. government's support of Israel.

Syria's conflict with Israel continued to shape its foreign policy. Since 1977 the Israelis had warned Assad not to exceed certain limits of activity in Leb-

Since assuming power in November 1970, Assad has considerably altered the nature of the Ba'th regime. After a short period of transition, it has become a presidential regime based on the personal leadership of Assad and on the entourage of his associates who control and operate the army, the party, and the security apparatus.
—ITAMAR RABINOVICH
Israeli historian

anon. Israel was raiding PLO strongholds in southern Lebanon on a regular basis, and Israeli leaders wanted no interference from Syria. For their part, Assad and his military command were deeply frustrated by Israel's involvement in Lebanon. They began to stage military maneuvers that seemed designed to distract Assad's opponents within Syria, boost the morale of his armed forces, and provoke the Israelis. All these goals were achieved, particularly the last. In late June 1979, Israeli jets shot down four Syrian planes in retaliation.

Tensions between Syria and Israel reached new heights over the next few years. In December 1981, the Israeli government announced that it was annexing the Golan Heights, the area it had captured from Syria during the 1967 war. Then, in the summer of 1982, Israel launched a second and larger invasion of Lebanon. Israeli strategists hoped that the offensive would wipe out PLO strongholds in Lebanon, push the Syrian army out of that country, and assist Lebanon's Maronite forces. Huge numbers of Lebanese and Palestinians were killed during the invasion, which also destroyed enormous amounts of property, especially in southern Lebanon and the Lebanese capital, Beirut. From an Israeli standpoint, important goals were achieved.

The wreckage of a Syrian air force jet lies in a field after a dogfight with Israeli jets over Lebanon in 1979. The presence of both the Syrian and Israeli armies in Lebanon led to several direct clashes between the two leading Middle Eastern military powers.

Syrian troops were driven out of several key positions, including Beirut; PLO bases in southern Lebanon and Beirut were destroyed; and Maronite leader Bashir Gemayel was elected Lebanon's president in September 1982.

For Assad, the Israeli invasion of Lebanon was a mixed blessing. On the one hand, Syria suffered serious casualties and the loss of many tanks, jets, and other war matériel. Assad had been tempted to escalate the conflict in order to try to recoup his losses, but he opted not to. He was well aware that in an all-out war, Syria would probably be badly defeated by Israel. On the other hand, despite Syria's losses in Lebanon, the invasion presented Assad with new opportunities. In May 1983, Lebanon signed a peace agreement with Israel that included terms for the withdrawal of Israeli troops from Lebanon. The accord called for the withdrawal of all Syrian forces, although some Israeli troops would remain in southern Lebanon so that Israel could secure its borders.

Soldiers of the Syrian-commanded Palestine Liberation Army prepare to withdraw to Damascus after being forced out of Lebanon by invading Israeli forces in the summer of 1982. The regular Syrian army was also expelled by the Israelis.

In part because the agreement had been reached without any Syrian participation, Assad refused to sign the accord or to agree to any of its main points. The Syrian regime stated bluntly that it was not going to consider withdrawal until all Israeli troops left Lebanon. Despite strong pressure exerted by the United States, which was also involved in the negotiations, Assad held to his position, thereby ruining the agreement's chances for success. In March 1984, President Amin Gemayel succumbed to Syrian pressure and annulled the accord. By that time Israel had already accepted the situation and withdrawn its troops to southern Lebanon.

By the end of 1983, Assad had accomplished a great deal in pulling Syria out of its isolation and reestablishing its importance as a power in the Middle East. Although tensions remained between the regime and the leaders of other Arab states, Assad had won new respect from allies and rivals alike. He had successfully stood up to Israel and the United States to demand a say in Lebanese affairs, once again insisting that he and his nation should play a dominant role in regional politics. It was increasingly apparent there would be no solution to the

A Palestinian woman sits among the ruins of a refugee camp in Lebanon in 1988 after a battle between pro-Syrian and pro-Arafat Palestinians. In the latter half of the 1980s, thousands of Palestinian civilians were killed by Israelis, Syrians, and the various Lebanese factions — and by other Palestinians.

Lebanese crisis or the Arab-Israeli conflict without Syrian cooperation.

Assad set out to exercise his renewed regional authority. Forcing the annulment of the Lebanese-Israeli agreement was only part of his overall approach to the Lebanese crisis. He was determined to see the conflict settled in a way that would ensure Syria a dominant role in Lebanese affairs. Toward this end, Assad adopted a new policy toward Lebanon beginning in 1984.

This approach aimed at establishing a new Lebanese political elite — one that had close ties to Syria. Assad attempted to undermine the position of the older, traditional leadership in Lebanon in favor of younger Druze, Shi'ite, and Maronite leaders. Through these new leaders, Assad hoped to reconcile the different Lebanese communities and bring stability to the war-torn country. He also hoped that these younger leaders would look to Syria for political guidance and support.

One of Assad's prime interests in Lebanon was gaining control of the Palestinian guerrilla organizations based there. In November 1983 he moved against Yasir Arafat in an attempt to end the rebel leader's independent guerrilla activity. Anti-Arafat PLO factions joined Syrian troops in attacking Arafat and his supporters in the northern Lebanese city of Tripoli. Arafat and approximately 4,000 of his followers were finally driven out of Tripoli following several violent battles. For Assad this was an important step in bringing the guerrilla movement under his influence, although Arafat would continue to be a thorn in the Syrian president's side.

November 1983 brought another, more sudden, change in Hafez al-Assad's fortunes. On November 13 he suffered a serious heart attack that left him hospitalized for three weeks. During the next six months Assad remained in poor health and was forced to leave the day-to-day governing of Syria to members of his regime. With the president recuperating in the background, a power struggle erupted in Damascus.

The conflict started when Rifat al-Assad tried to assume his brother's role as head of state. His bid for supremacy was immediately challenged by top-level army commanders who remained loyal to President Assad. In February 1984, soldiers from Rifat's Defense Companies exchanged shots with regular army units near the presidential palace in Damascus.

Although he was still recuperating, Hafez al-Assad was forced to step in. He had one of the Defense Companies' senior commanders arrested, and the immediate threat of a coup was averted. To placate his brother, the president appointed Rifat as one of Syria's three vice-presidents on March 11. But Assad knew that Rifat would not be long content with this token position. Unless he took decisive action, an armed confrontation between the Defense Companies and the regular army seemed inevitable.

In May, Assad sent Rifat to Moscow, the capital of the Soviet Union, as part of a diplomatic delegation. Rifat was not allowed to return to Syria until six months later. During his brother's absence, Assad reassigned many of the officers who had supported Rifat's takeover attempt, reduced the number of Defense Company units from 60 to 15, and incorporated these remaining units into the

We shall chase them [opponents] at home and abroad. . . . We are prepared to exterminate a million citizens in order to ensure safety and defend the revolution.

—RIFAT AL-ASSAD in 1980, five days after a grenade had been thrown at his brother Hafez al-Assad

regular army. But Rifat al-Assad's bid for power had earned him the vice-presidency, a position that brought him a measure of political respectability. According to Assad biographer Moshe Ma'oz, the Syrian president was motivated by more than family loyalty when he decided to treat his upstart brother so gently. "Assad recognized Rifat as an important factor in his delicate security apparatus," Ma'oz theorized. "Rifat has not only done the dirty work for Assad by brutally suppressing the opposition, but his well-equipped troops are the guardians of some of the most sensitive centers of the regime, and are capable of counterbalancing or overpowering regular military units which one day might try to topple Assad."

By 1985, Assad was firmly back in power after parliament passed a vote of confidence in his leadership and a popular referendum for the presidency — in which he was the sole candidate — gave him a reported 99.9 percent of votes cast. The question of his successor was shelved, and Hafez al-Assad was able to return to the business of governing Syria and influencing policy throughout the Mideast.

The ongoing Lebanese civil war continued to be one of his prime concerns. Since it first intervened in 1976, Assad's regime has periodically changed its allegiances in an attempt to influence the course

Lebanese president Amin Gemayel confers with Assad in 1984. Although Syria remained isolated from other Middle Eastern states, Assad was recognized as a pivotal broker in efforts to settle the various conflicts in the Middle East.

As the 1980s drew to a close, Assad had held power for nearly two full decades. Although his presidency was marked by warfare, tangled military involvements on foreign soil, and cruel repression at home, he had transformed Syria into an assertive and important Middle Eastern power.

of Lebanon's chaotic political scene. Hoping to end the strife once and for all, Assad brought together Druze, Shi'ite, and Christian leaders to sign an accord in 1985. The peace plan faltered after the Christian commander who endorsed the agreement was driven out of Lebanon by rival Christian factions. This spelled an end to the Syrian-sponsored pact, but Assad continued to strive to end Lebanon's civil war — and to expand his influence in the country.

President Assad made another attempt to resolve the Lebanese conflict in 1988. In September of that year the country's Christian president, Amin Gemayel, left office, and the national legislature was unable to agree on a new leader to replace him. To fill the power vacuum, the departing Gemayel appointed a Christian army commander, General Michel Aoun, to head an interim military government. Muslim leaders objected to this arrangement, charging that it violated the power-sharing arrangement that had governed Lebanese politics since independence. Hoping to formulate a settlement that would please all sides, Assad met with American diplomat Richard Murphy. The two men decided to propose that Mikhail al-Daher, a member of Lebanon's parliament, become Lebanon's new head of state. This plan failed when Christian forces rejected Daher's candidacy on the grounds that he was Assad's puppet.

In the absence of an accord, Lebanon has developed two rival governments — one Christian, one Muslim. Relations between the two factions are generally hostile, and no compromise is in sight. Muslim leaders, many of whom are aligned with Assad, seek to end Israel's influence in the country; Christian forces, supported by the Israelis, demand the withdrawal of Syrian troops from Lebanese territory. Any possible resolution of the civil war is further complicated by factional infighting and the demands of Palestinian organizations.

Assad's other primary foreign policy concern, the Arab-Israeli conflict, also remained unresolved in the late 1980s. At the heart of this conflict is the fate of the Palestinian people. In December of 1987 the Palestinians in the areas occupied by Israel in the 1967 war — the West Bank and Gaza — rose up against Israeli rule. These Palestinians demanded an end to the occupation and the establishment of an independent state. Although the uprising (the Intifadah) precipitated a flurry of activity on the part of Arab, Israeli, and American diplomats, the leaders of Israel have refused to negotiate on the Palestinian demands, and the solution to this decades-old conflict remains elusive.

As the 1980s draw to a close, Assad faces challenges at home as well as abroad. Although he has withstood dozens of attempts to unseat him, opposition to his regime continues. Assad's power is still based primarily on the strength of the armed forces and his intelligence networks. Outside of the Alawi community and the Ba'th party, the president has little support. Syria's Sunni population remains generally hostile to what it sees as an authoritarian regime run by the Alawi minority it has long distrusted.

Assad's capacity to win at least the grudging acceptance of the general Syrian population will be one measure historians will use to judge his effectiveness as a ruler. Up until 1989 his record in this area has been poor. This issue will affect the rest of Assad's presidency. It will also determine whether or not the Ba'th regime remains in power after Assad leaves office — and whether the years after his departure will be a time of calm or of upheaval.

Much depends on Hafez al-Assad, the quiet, reserved leader who has stirred up the passions of the Middle East and the world at large. That he has had a lasting impact on Syria and the entire Middle East is undeniable. He has built a strong presidential regime in a nation marked by political chaos and has managed to stay in power longer than any of his predecessors. During his tenure as Syria's president, he has transformed his nation from a poor, isolated country into an influential and assertive nation. His attempts to modernize his country and unite the Arab world have been hampered by the complex realities of Middle Eastern politics, but Assad remains determined to achieve his goals.

It is doubtful whether his successor would be capable of sustaining Assad's remarkable achievements, particularly rendering Syria such an unprecedented stability, and making her, for the first time, a regional power in the Middle East.
—MOSHE MA'OZ
Assad biographer

Further Reading

Abd Allah, Umar F. *The Islamic Struggle in Syria.* Berkeley, CA: Mizan Press, 1983.

Antonius, George. *The Arab Awakening.* London: Hamish Hamilton Ltd., 1969.

Devlin, John. *The Ba'th Party: A History from Its Origins to 1966.* Stanford, CA: Hoover Institution Press, 1976.

———. *Syria: Modern State in an Ancient Land.* Boulder, CO: Westview Press, 1983.

Drysdale, Alasdair. "The Asad Regime" *MERIP Reports,* No. 110 November-December 1982.

Goldschmidt, Arthur. *A Concise History of the Middle East.* Boulder, CO: Westview Press, 1979.

Hudson, Michael C. *Arab Politics: The Search for Legitimacy.* New Haven, CT: Yale University Press, 1977.

Khadduri, Majid. *Arab Personalities in Politics.* Washington, DC: The Middle East Institute, 1981.

Ma'oz, Moshe. *Asad: The Sphinx of Damascus.* New York: Weidenfeld & Nicolson, 1988.

———. "Profile: Hafiz al-Asad of Syria" *Orbis,* Summer 1987.

Mitchell, Richard P. *The Society of Muslim Brothers.* London: Oxford University Press, 1969.

Rabinovitch, Itamar. *Syria Under the Ba'th 1963–66: The Army-Party Symbiosis.* Jerusalem: Israel Universities Press, 1972.

Petran, Tabitha. *The Struggle Over Lebanon.* New York: Monthly Review Press, 1987.

Seale, Patrick. *Asad of Syria: The Struggle for the Middle East.* London: I.B. Tauris & Co. Ltd., 1988.

———. *The Struggle for Syria.* London: Oxford University Press, 1965.

Tibawi, Abdul-Latif. *A Modern History of Syria Including Lebanon and Palestine.* London: Macmillan, 1969.

van Dam, Nikolaos. *The Struggle for Power in Syria.* New York: St. Martin's Press, 1979.

Chronology

1930   Born Abu Sulayman (name later changed to Hafez al-Assad) on October 6 in Qardaha, Syria

1946   Syria gains independence from France

1947   The Ba'th party is founded

1948   State of Israel created; Syria joins in an unsuccessful Arab invasion of Israel

1952   Assad enters the Military Academy

1954   Transfers to the Air Force Academy

1957   Receives specialized military training in the Soviet Union

1958   Egypt and Syria form the United Arab Republic (UAR)

1961   Syria withdraws from the UAR; Assad and other members of the Ba'thist Military Committee arrested for opposition activities and released after two months; Assad takes post at the department of transportation

1963   The Ba'thist Revolution

1964   Assad named head of the Syrian air force

1966   Imprisoned once again for opposition activities; Syrian government under Amin al-Hafez is overthrown by Salah Jadid; Assad becomes minister of defense

1967   The Six-Day War between Israel and the Arabs

1970   Assad overthrows Jadid and assumes power over Syria

1973   Syria joins forces with Egypt in an attack on Israel

1976   Assad sends forces into Lebanon in an unsuccessful attempt to end the civil war

1979   Egyptian president Anwar Sadat and Israeli leader Menachem Begin sign the Camp David agreement in Washington, D.C.; Syria severs relations with Egypt

1980   Border confrontations occur between Syria and Jordan; Syria signs Friendship Treaty with the Soviet Union; assassination attempt on Assad fails

1982   The Assad regime crushes the popular uprising in Hama; Israel invades Lebanon; Syrian forces clash with Israeli troops

1983   Assad suffers heart attack; succession struggle ensues

1985   Assad regains control of government

1988   Lebanon's president, Amin Gemayel, a Christian, resigns; two rival governments develop as result of power struggle between Christian and Muslim forces

Index

Matthew S. Gordon was born in Princeton, New Jersey, and grew up in Beirut, Lebanon, where his parents taught at the American University of Beirut. He received his B.A. in history from Drew University in 1979 and is currently enrolled at Columbia University, where he is working toward his Ph.D. in Middle Eastern studies.

Arthur M. Schlesinger, jr., taught history at Harvard for many years and is currently Albert Schweitzer Professor of the Humanities at City University of New York. He is the author of numerous highly praised works in American history and has twice been awarded the Pulitzer Prize. He served in the White House as special assistant to Presidents Kennedy and Johnson.

PLAINSBORO PUBLIC LIBRARY
641 Plainsboro Road
Plainsboro, NJ 08536